A Five Part Plan for Patent Reform

A FIVE PART PLAN FOR PATENT REFORM

CHARLES DUAN

A PK THINKS WHITE PAPER

Copyright © 2014 Public Knowledge. This work is licensed under the Creative Commons Attribution-ShareAlike 4.0 International License. To view a copy of this license, visit http://creativecommons.org/licenses/by-sa/4.0/.

Print edition, 2014. The original edition is available at http://www.publicknowledge.org/documents/a-five-part-plan-for-patent-reform.

Published by:
Public Knowledge
1818 N Street NW, Suite 410
Washington, DC 20036
http://publicknowledge.org

Images: William B. Hargrave, U.S. Pat. No. 765,361, Device for Eradicating Facial Wrinkles, filed Nov. 12, 1903. Charles A. Miller, U.S. Pat. No. 1,542,568, Radio Dial Adjuster, filed Dec. 29, 1922. Walter S. Olson, U.S. Pat. No. 964,803, Flying Toy Bird, filed Apr. 12, 1909. Charles G. Purdy, U.S. Pat. No. 1,466,559, Exercising Device, filed Mar. 29, 1921. John C. Raymond, U.S. Pat. No. 627,351, Bicycle, filed Nov. 4, 1897.

PKthinks

The patent system is an important motivator for new technology. But in its present state, the patent system has problems and loopholes that allow for abuse and exploitation, harming rather than promoting innovation.

In this white paper, we look at how to fix those problems in patent law, by identifying areas that are currently abused and that require reform. Those five areas are:

Accounting for all inventors. The standards for patenting must account for all types of inventors, large and small, and especially those who work outside the patent system.

Clarity of patents. Patents are intended to disseminate knowledge about new inventions and technologies. Thus, patent documents must be made clear and understandable, so that they serve that function.

Targeting the right parties. Threats of complex patent litigation, levied against consumers, small companies, and non-technology businesses, stifle innovation without any corresponding benefit to inventors.

Avoiding gamesmanship in litigation. Licensing and enforcement of patents should be about the merits of the patents, not about a party's ability to run its opponents into the ground with litigation costs.

Maintaining competition in the innovation economy. Patent owners ought to use their patents in ways consistent with long-standing principles favoring a competitive marketplace.

Contents

1 Introduction — 1
  1.1 A Generally Good System, But Often Abused — 2
  1.2 Five Areas for Reform — 3

2 Background on the Patent System — 5
  2.1 The Theory of Patents — 5
  2.2 Obtaining and Using a Patent — 6
  2.3 The Role of the Troll — 7

3 Accounting for All Inventors — 9
  3.1 Computer Software Startups — 9
  3.2 Open Innovation Communities — 10
  3.3 Alternative Rewards for Invention — 11
  3.4 Conflicts Between the Incentives — 12
  3.5 Finding the Right Balance — 13
  3.6 Improving Patent Quality — 14

4 Clarity of Patents — 17
  4.1 Judicial Interpretations of Patent Language — 20
  4.2 Patent Examination Procedures — 20
  4.3 Limiting the Volume Game — 21
  4.4 Improved Technological Tools — 21

5 Targeting the Right Parties — 23
  5.1 Nineteenth Century Patent Trolls — 23
  5.2 Redirecting Patent Suits to Manufacturers — 25
  5.3 Customer Suit Exception — 26
  5.4 Abolishing Software Patents Is Insufficient — 26

6	**Avoiding Gamesmanship in Litigation**	**29**
	6.1 Demand Letters	29
	6.2 Fair Notice to Patent Defendants	30
	6.3 Costs of Litigation Procedures	31
	6.4 Reasonable Royalty Computations	33
	6.5 Alternatives to Litigation	34
	6.6 Leveling the Playing Field	35
7	**Maintaining Competition in the Innovation Economy**	**37**
	7.1 FRAND Obligations	37
	7.2 Patent Holdup	38
8	**Conclusion: The Future of Patents**	**41**
A	**Notes**	**45**
B	**Bibliography**	**73**

1 Introduction

PATENTS ARE SIMULTANEOUSLY one of the most obscure and one of the most contentious areas of the law. "Even Rube Goldberg couldn't have invented anything as confused and perverse as America's patent and intellectual property protection system," said one scholar, comparing the patent system to the artist "famous for crafting machines of ridiculous complexity."[1] That complexity has not stopped numerous efforts for reform, with members of Congress introducing eleven patent-related bills in 2013.[2]

One would think that this esotericity and contention would leave no room for agreement on patent policy. But there is one area of widespread agreement: patents are one of the most abused areas of the law. The term "patent troll," coined by a lawyer in the early 2000s, is well known in the general lexicon to refer to an entity who produces no products of its own but rather asserts patents, often patents on inventions that the entity did not itself invent, against companies who do produce new technologies and products.[3] Criticisms of patent trolls, and of the patent system that gives rise to them, abound.

These accounts of abuses by patent trolls are neither hypothetical nor academic. The harms to small businesses, innovators, and the economy are well documented and empirically researched. One report documented that small companies had stalled product development, delayed hiring new employees, or even gone out of business as a result of patent assertion.[4] Another widely-cited study estimated the direct costs of patent assertion by non-practicing entities (that is, companies that exist solely to assert patents) at $29 billion in 2011, with $10.8 billion of that coming from small- or medium-sized firms.[5] Patent litigation is big business, making it an attractive target to those wanting to abuse it.

Although there are abuses, it is also necessary to account for the important purposes and values that underlie the patent system. By providing the reward of a patent, patents give inventors an incentive to research and develop new inventions, and also give those inventors some lead time in bringing products to market.[6] Without patents, the theory goes, small inventors would never spend time inventing, since large companies could sweep in, copy the inventions, and undercut the small inventors' businesses. And certainly many inventions through history, such as the light bulb, the airplane, and the photocopier, were invented by small inventors and protected by patents.[7]

To find the right direction for policy reform of the patent system, it is necessary first to reconcile these two competing threads, of the value patents have created and the harm they are causing.

1.1 A Generally Good System, But Often Abused

These two divergent views of the patent system, as destroyer of small businesses and as engine of innovation, have led to wildly different and apparently irreconcilable views of that patent system. On the one hand, some have called the system fundamentally flawed and advocated for the abolition of patents altogether.[8] Others have defended the need to protect inventors at all costs and opposed any changes that might upset or potentially weaken patents.[9]

But both of these views seem overly simplistic, and unfair to a complex system such as patents. The question is whether there is an adequate middle ground, where the benefits of the patent system can be maintained and even enhanced, while the drawbacks can be removed.

At the most basic level, the answer to resolving these conflicting views on the patent system seems to be this: there is a core of patents that is useful and valuable to society. That core has been surrounded by layers and layers of abusive practices, clever lawyering, and moneyed interests to turn the patent system into something entirely different.

The question, then, is how to separate out that valuable core from the layers of abuse. The simplest way to do so is to focus on the abuses that are currently occurring, and to categorize those so that they may be attacked individually. It is not difficult to find examples of those abuses, ranging from shotgun lawsuit campaigns targeted against small retail and service

A Five Part Plan for Patent Reform

businesses, to overbroad patents stretched to cover basic ideas in technology, to monopolistic arrangements intended to keep out competition. The remaining discussion, then, will review these abusive practices within the patent system, and propose reforms to curb those practices, within the framework of our five-part focus for patent reform.

1.2 Five Areas for Reform

This white paper thus identifies five key areas in which the patent system is ripe for reform. These areas were selected based on current patent reform considerations, concerns raised by academics and the general public, and general considerations of policy and consumer interests. The areas are:

- **Accounting for all inventors.** Patents are not the only stimulus for invention and innovation. Numerous technology creators, such as computer software startups, open innovation communities, and academia, have other incentives to flourish, discover, and advance science and technology. These non-patent incentives should be celebrated, and not weakened by overbroad protection of patents.

- **Clarity of patents.** The grant of a patent is intended to disclose knowledge in exchange for a temporary monopoly over a certain class of inventions. This relies on clarity in two areas: (1) clarity in the description of the invention, so that others may learn from it, and (2) clarity in the description of the monopoly, so that others may know what is covered and what is not. Where a patent uses imprecise language and fuzzy boundaries, that patent may easily be abused and thus disserves the public.

- **Targeting the right parties.** Traditionally, patents were the domain of big technology companies, and the structure of patent acquisition and enforcement grew around that domain. Today, however, patent lawsuits fall on the doorsteps of small businesses and customers of technologies, parties who do not expect to be part of the patent game and are ill equipped to play. This provides an opportunity for abusers of the system to take advantage of unwary and unsuspecting consumers.

- **Avoiding gamesmanship in litigation.** Patent lawsuits are complicated and expensive. Much of this complexity and expense is necessary and expected, because the technologies are advanced, and the product markets at stake are large. But clever litigants can exacerbate this complexity, hoping to win cases not on the merits but rather on exhaustion and cost.

- **Maintaining competition in the innovation economy.** Because patents are a temporary monopoly, they necessarily and appropriately are an exception to the general view that competition is preferable to monopoly. But the inclination of any monopoly holder is to expand that monopoly beyond its anticipated reach. Thus, patent owners have attempted to use patents to hold up technology, block adoption of interconnection standards, and otherwise create undesirable anticompetitive situations.

These five areas for reform are interrelated, and many proposed reforms will deal with more than one area. But each of these five areas is independent, and solving one will not automatically solve others. There is no silver bullet to patent reform, and improving the patent system will require a long-term, multifaceted effort. But that effort is worth the potential innovation and creation that a well-crafted patent system will bring about.

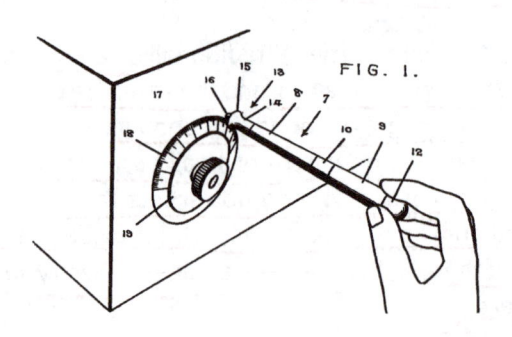

2 Background on the Patent System

BECAUSE THE PATENT SYSTEM is a fairly complex and unusual area of the law, some background may be needed for those without much familiarity with patents. This section will discuss the basic theory behind why patents are issued, and then look at the mechanics of how patents are obtained and used.

2.1 The Theory of Patents

"Intellectual property" is the term applied to various legal systems in which entities are given exclusive rights over non-tangible things. In the United States, as summarized in Table 1, there are generally three main types of intellectual property, which are generally distinguishable by the type of non-tangible things to which the exclusive rights are given. Copyrights cover creative works, such as books, music, and artwork. Trademarks cover names that are attached to products and services, such as brand names and logos. Patents cover inventions, such as machines, processes, and systems. The focus here, of course, is patents.

Table 1 Summary of major types of intellectual property.

Type	What covered	Exclusive rights
Copyright	Creative works	Copying, distribution, public performance, etc.
Trademark	Product identifiers	Use in commerce
Patent	Inventions	Making, using, selling, etc.

5

The basic theory behind patents is that they provide an incentive for inventors to invent. A person might come up with a great idea for a new machine for shelling peanuts, say, but it might take a lot of time, money, research, and development to turn that idea into a marketable product or service. But once the shelling machine was on the market, then others could copy it and undercut the price.[10]

Without patents, the shelling machine inventor would probably do one of two things: (1) not spend the time and money in developing the shelling machine, choosing to do something else; or (2) operate the machine in a secret factory, not allowing anyone to see it. Neither of these two options is particularly desirable.[11] The first one means that fewer new inventions would be created, and the second option means that other inventors will not be able to improve on the invention.[12]

Thus, patents provide a way out of this dilemma. A patent offers the patent owner the exclusive right to make, use, or sell the invention,[13] as a *quid pro quo* for the inventor revealing to the world how the invention works in a written document called a patent specification.[14] Thus, inventors will have the incentives to invest time and resources into inventing (solving the first problem), and the public will have the benefit of the advancement in knowledge (solving the second problem).[15]

That last part is the key: patents are issued to advance the public's interest in knowledge and access to new technologies. Patents should encourage inventors to create and reveal new inventions for the benefit of everyone. This sentiment is in fact embodied right in the Constitution of the United States, which authorizes Congress to grant patents in order to "promote the Progress of Science and useful Arts."[16] Even Thomas Jefferson, the first patent examiner of the U.S. Patent Office, saw "the exclusive right to invention as given not of natural right, but for the benefit of society."[17]

2.2 Obtaining and Using a Patent

To obtain a patent, an inventor submits a patent application to the U.S. Patent and Trademark Office. The patent application includes two parts. The *specification*, which usually includes drawings and text, should describe the invention in sufficient detail so that readers can recognize the inventor's contribution and learn how to reconstruct it.[18] The *claims*, which are the numbered paragraphs at the end of the patent document, are the legal definition of the patent right.[19] Just as a title deed to a plot of land specifies the metes and bounds of the property, the claims specify the metes and bounds of what infringes and what does not infringe the patent.[20]

The Patent Office will then examine the application. This includes reviewing the prior art: the examiner will search for similar patents, technical papers, and other information that predates the application, and try to find one that is sufficiently similar to the claims of the application.[21] If such prior art is found, then the examiner will reject the application, and offer the applicant a chance to respond.[22] Often the examiner and the applicant will go through several rounds of exchanges and revisions to the patent application, until the examiner is satisfied and agrees to allow the application.[23] Then the Patent Office issues a patent to the applicant.[24]

With patent in hand, the patent owner (called a "patentee") can now use the patent, up until the patent term expires, to sue others who infringe the patent.[25] Another party infringes a patent if they make, sell, use, offer to sell, or import something that comes within the claims of the patent.[26] Often the patent owner and the accused infringer disagree what the patent claims mean, so this is resolved by the court hearing the lawsuit, in a procedure called "claim construction."[27] Upon deciding the meaning of the patent claims and other issues, the court can decide whether the accused party infringes the patent. If so, then the court can award money to the patent owner, order the infringer to stop conducting the infringing activity, or both.[28]

2.3 The Role of the Troll

Patent trolls are an arguably new phenomenon that have arisen in the last few decades.[29] The term "patent troll" generally refers, to varying degrees, to an entity that asserts patents without producing any products or offering any services based on those patents. There is obviously a great deal of uncertainty in what constitutes a patent troll, and authors have proposed various alternate terms and definitions, such as "non-practicing entity" (NPE), "patent assertion entity" (PAE), and "patent monetizing entity" (PME), to name a few.[30]

The rhetoric around patent reform often focuses on the harms of patent trolls and suggests a need to target those entities and their practices. And, indeed, there are good reasons to believe that when an entity does not actually put its patents into use, that entity is substantially more likely to engage in undesirable and abusive behaviors. For example, entities that do not practice their patents lack the incentive to truly educate the public about their inventions,[31] but rather they may prefer to wait for others to come up with those inventions independently and then spring up demanding a license fee. Also, patent trolls lack business relationships with manufacturers and other industry players, and are thus free to engage in abusive business practices without fear of repercussions.[32]

But patent trolls are symptomatic of broader problems with the patent system overall. Because the system permits abusive practices, it is not surprising that a business model has grown to take advantage of and profit from those abuses. But those abuses can continue to exist and to be used whether or not patent trolls are present—and, indeed, some evidence suggests that even operating, product-producing companies engage in the same sorts of abusive practices ordinarily ascribed to patent trolls.[33]

Thus, efforts to reform the patent system ought not to focus on defining and opposing patent trolls as a business model. Rather, efforts should be targeted at rooting out the loopholes, problems, and abuses of the system overall. When patent trolls are given nothing to take advantage of in the patent system, they will naturally wither away, and we will be left with a stronger system that promotes innovation and progress.

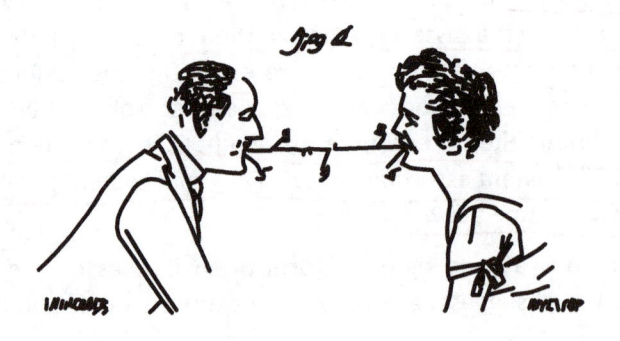

3 Accounting for All Inventors

THE TRADITIONAL RATIONALE behind the issuance of patents is utilitarian: by granting limited monopolies on inventions, the government can incentivize individuals and firms to spend resources on inventing. The limited monopoly, namely the right to exclude others from practicing the invention for a period of time, both gives a financial reward to those who invent and grants an opportunity for them to commercialize their inventions without interference from competitors.[34]

The empirical evidence for this rationale is mixed. The area in which the patent incentive most clearly succeeds is in the pharmaceutical industry,[35] but some have suggested that this is primarily the case because of artificially imposed regulatory requirements that necessitate the exclusive lead time offered by patents.[36] In other fields of technology, surveys and other evidence have suggested that the patent incentive is insubstantial or vastly ignored.[37]

In any event, it is unnecessary to consider in too much depth the empirical evidence for the patent incentive, because it is certainly not the only incentive for innovation. The fast-paced startup community, open source software, the prestige of publication, and prizes and rewards for new discoveries, among other things, are all alternative incentives for innovation beyond patents, as explained below.[38]

3.1 Computer Software Startups

The widespread use of the Internet and computer technologies has led to a proliferation in small software startups. The market of mobile device applications, for example, is globally valued at over $53 billion[39] and accounts for approximately 466,000 jobs created since 2007.[40] Many of the major Internet companies today have their roots in such a small business.[41]

Small software technology startups often do not rely on patents for protecting their innovations. With patent applications costing about $25,000 to file and prosecute,[42] they are well beyond the financial reach of these small startups that may not even have $25,000 to run their business in the first year.[43] Yet the number of such startups is proof that there is sufficient incentive to innovate in that arena even without patents.

Instead, different incentives predominate. The first mover advantage is particularly valuable in the fast-paced world of computer software.[44] Network effects hold strongly with software, as adopters of a company's technology are less likely to move to competitive offerings due to built-up social networks, cost of converting data, and familiarity with user interfaces.[45] Additionally, software companies are prone to failure for numerous reasons, so many software engineers are comfortable with frequent "pivots" to entirely new ideas.[46] The mere experience of starting a software company, say many such engineers, is incentive enough to innovate even in the face of daunting odds, as it is easy and nearly cost-free to abandon one idea and move on to the next.

3.2 Open Innovation Communities

Open innovation communities are collectives of individuals and entities who openly share their innovations, making those innovations available to others for use, adaptation, and improvement.[47] Although the open source software community is perhaps the best known of these, open innovation communities may be found in many other areas of technology besides software development, including electronic hardware manufacturing, 3D printing, biology, and environmental engineering.[48]

To strong proponents of the patent incentive theory, open source software and related models of innovation present a quandary: how can innovation occur in a world where products are given away for free and competitors are allowed—even encouraged—to copy? Yet widespread use and constant improvement of open source software suggests that those incentives must still be present. Some of the most widely used software programs today, including the GNU/Linux operating system, the Apache HTTP server, and the Firefox web browser, were developed by the open source community.

Indeed, scholars have documented those alternative incentives that have contributed to the growth of the open source software and other communities. Reputation benefits play a significant role: as one seminal work put it in describing two popular software projects, "by properly rewarding the egos of many other hackers, a strong developer/coordinator can use the Internet to capture the benefits of having lots of co-developers."[49] Companies like IBM and Red Hat invest in open source development to accrue returns such as consulting services.[50] And basic ideals of sharing and disseminating knowledge motivate others.[51] Thus, a variety of incentives, entirely apart from the patent incentive, can spur innovation within open innovation communities.

3.3 Alternative Rewards for Invention

Patents are one type of reward for innovation, but there are many others. Prizes for innovation have been suggested as a solution to the economic inefficiency of patent monopolies. "The alternative of awarding prizes would be more efficient and more equitable," writes one prominent economist.[52] And numerous prizes are granted to incentivize societal progress: Alfred Nobel, for example, bequeathed his fortune to establish prizes awarded to "those who, during the preceding year, shall have conferred the greatest benefit to mankind."[53]

There are many examples of rewards for innovation, beyond the straightforward prize. Academics are rewarded for their ideas and discoveries by having their papers accepted in journals. Foundations run competitions for the first person to solve an unsolved problem, to encourage inventors to develop creative solutions. Governments provide tax incentives for research and development. And researchers with new ideas can apply for grants, both government and privately-funded, to pursue those ideas.[54]

An example of the last of these types of rewards incentivizing innovation may be found in the development of the Internet. Many Internet technologies were built under federal grants,[55] which incidentally restricted acquisition of patents on the technology.[56] Further Internet development was supervised by standards organizations like the W3C, which expressly disallows patenting of technology adopted into standards.[57] The reward of a federal grant or incorporation into an Internet standard was sufficient to bring about incredible technological development without the use of patents.

Certainly none of these alternate incentives can entirely supplant the patent system, as each person is motivated by different incentives. What is important, though, is that no single type of incentive is the sole or predominant engine of new innovation and technology.

3.4 Conflicts Between the Incentives

While, in an ideal world, all of these incentives would complement each other to maximize invention, in reality these incentives conflict and sometimes work at opposing purposes. The focus here is particularly on how the patent incentive can conflict with other incentives to innovate, and how reforms to the patent system can reduce these conflicts.

For example, the first mover advantage is an incentive for startup entrepreneurs, and that incentive is undercut when second movers or even non-movers acquire and assert patents. Thus, there is substantial anecdotal evidence of innovative software startups dropping products or closing shop altogether in the face of patent threats.[58]

The interference between patents and open source software is also well known. One study from 2004 has shown that the Linux kernel, a popular and widely-used open source program, potentially infringes 283 patents.[59] Indeed, when a bundle of 882 patents were proposed to be sold in 2011, the Department of Justice intervened out of concern that the patents would "jeopardize the ability of open-source software, such as Linux, to continue to innovate and compete."[60] Similarly, the authors of the GNU General Public License are of the view that patents "obstruct free software development," which led to the inclusion of a mandatory patent license in the most recent version of the GPL.[61]

There is also a conflict between the patent incentive and incentives of alternate rewards. Patents can interfere with the ability of scholars to conduct research, thereby diminishing the ability of academia to pursue innovative ideas. However, this example is instructive, because patent law already provides an accommodation for this conflict: an exception for experimental use. That doctrine, which exempts from patent infringement non-commercial experimental uses of patented inventions,[62] accommodates those who invent to obtain public or academic recognition. Additionally instructive, however, is the degree to which this experimental use doctrine has been narrowed over time,[63] reflecting an unfortunate shift in the relative valuation between the patent incentive and rewards-based research incentives.

3.5 Finding the Right Balance

One task for patent reform, then, is to consider adjustments to the patent system that better accommodate these alternate incentives for innovation. The goal of such adjustments is to better encourage these inventors incentivized by factors other than patents, and to ensure that patents do not stand in the way of those inventors.

Consider the following ideas for recalibrating the patent system in view of these alternate incentives and alternate inventors.

For one thing, the standards for granting patents should be reconsidered. Many aspects of the current patent system reflect an assumption that patents are the primary driver of innovation, and modern developments challenge that assumption. This question of patent quality is discussed in Section 3.6.

Along similar lines, patent law includes an old doctrine called "experimental use," which protects those who engage in experimentation from the risk of patent infringement.[64] However, over the years courts have sharply narrowed the availability of the experimental use exception, exactly at a time when more and more experimentation is occurring, on the part of consumers, home inventors, and other small parties. Expansion of this doctrine could provide protection to that grassroots innovation that could otherwise be threatened by patents.

Additionally, some have considered the possibility of using specially-configured patent licenses to promote open innovation rather than interfere with it. The idea is that a properly crafted license agreement attached to a patent could encourage others to share knowledge rather than hold it closed behind patents, in the same way that copyright licenses like the GPL and Creative Commons licenses encourage others to share creative works.

One such proposal, the Defensive Patent License (DPL), institutes a system by which an entity may agree not to assert its patents against other

DPL members, and in exchange the entity receives an automatic, free license to all other patents under the DPL.[65] Thus, the DPL "blends the general strategy of defensive patenting with the [open innovation community] values of openness and freedom" to "provide an interoperable, technologically neutral, reliable, and legally binding commitment to defense."[66] Proposals like these take the patent system, which is built around the singular patent incentive, and turn it around to incentivize other values shared by different kinds of inventors.[67]

3.6 Improving Patent Quality

A common complaint about the patent system is the number of "low-quality" patents that are issued.[68] There are frequent reports of patents on old or obvious ideas, particularly in the field of software.[69] Many people believe that these poor quality patents are the root of the problems that the patent system faces today. They thus call for better examination of patents through increased funding to the Patent Office, better training of examiners, and longer time for examination.[70]

Improving patent quality is a key component of accounting for all inventors and innovators. The process of invention is incremental,[71] so inventors depend on a pool of knowledge not encumbered by patents, on which their inventions may be based. Part of this pool comes from unpatentable abstract ideas, laws of nature, and physical phenomena, which the Supreme Court has described as "part of the storehouse of knowledge of all men...free to all men and reserved exclusively to none."[72] Another part of this pool comes from old technologies in the prior art,[73] as well as the knowledge that would be obvious to a "person having ordinary skill in the art."[74] If a patent erroneously issues on a technology within that public pool, or if courts misread the boundaries of the pool too narrowly, then future innovators and future innovation are hindered.[75]

The need to account for all inventors extends to many areas of the patent quality problem. Patent examination is one such area. The Patent Office traditionally searched for prior art primarily in the library of past patents,[76] but today, where so much innovation occurs outside of the patent system, the Patent Office is starting to seek out external sources of information to discover prior art.[77]

The basic standard for patent quality is another area where accounting for all inventors must play a role. The Supreme Court recognized this in the case *KSR International Co. v. Teleflex Inc.*[78] For many years, the courts had used a test for what would be obvious to a person of ordinary skill in the art, namely that some "teaching, suggestion, or motivation" to combine two different ideas must exist before the combination could be deemed obvious.[79] The Supreme Court rejected that test, based on its reasoning that the "diversity of inventive pursuits and of modern technology counsels against limiting the analysis" to that test—that is, because the test failed to account for all types of inventors and technology.[80] Nevertheless, the requirement for some sort of motivation to combine even persists after *KSR*.[81]

That conflict between the "motivation to combine" test and actual inventors is placed sharply in focus when considering open-source software developers, for example. Non-proprietary software developers and other innovation communities value interoperability and combinability of software. Thus, the legal assumption that new combinations are uncommon and often worthy of patents conflicts with the experiences of those software developers, for whom new combinations are routine and expected. Uncorrected, this mismatch means that patents would likely stifle rather than encourage the tinkering and exploration that drives many innovators today.

A critical step in improving patent quality, then, is accounting for the ways in which all types of inventors work and innovate. The Patent Office and the courts need to know how a "person having ordinary skill in the art" approaches problem solving and invention. Without sufficient contact with actual innovators of all types, these decisionmaking bodies will not be able to craft patent policy that promotes innovation for all.

So it is important for these decisionmakers to reach out to inventing communities, even those that do not file for patents, and it is important for those communities to reach out to the Patent Office and other decisionmakers.[82] Indeed, the White House and Patent Office have initiated several programs to obtain input on patent policy,[83] and these initiatives should be continued and broadened to reach the whole innovating community.

4 Clarity of Patents

AMONG THE MOST COMMON COMPLAINTS about the patent system is that patents are impossible to read. Patent documents are filled with complex language that often, to the lay reader or technical engineer, appears confusing or even misleading.[84]

It is no surprise, then, that those with technical but not legal skill do not find patents to be a useful source of technical information. One survey of researchers in the nanotechnology field found found numerous complaints on the usefulness of patents as technical disclosures.[85] Among the surveyed researchers, 36% never read patents, many of them complaining about "the style in which patents are written—patents were called 'vague,' 'legal jargon,' 'incomprehensible,' and lacking 'technical detail.' "[86] Those who had read patents had similar complaints: "To a scientist," an academic chemist wrote, "the patent literature looks like an invention of lawyers for the benefit of other patent lawyers."[87] Only 38% of surveyed researchers believed that one could reproduce an invention from the patent specification—a clear indication that disclosure and dissemination of knowledge, the cornerstone goals of the patent system, are not being served.[88]

Those outside of academic circles have expressed the most concern about the difficulty of understanding patents and particularly patent claims. One author, in describing how to read patent claims, laments that they are "a dense form of legal English," further explaining that the "drafting of patent claims is a black art" because claims are "full of magic words."[89] "Patents are so vague," one attorney said, that "[i]f someone claims infringement, the only way to resolve it is through litigating."[90] Where litigation is "the only way" to assess the meaning of a patent, that patent has failed to serve its public notice function.

This lack of clarity in patents is particularly unfortunate given the intention that patents are meant to serve, namely as disclosures to the world of new inventions and discoveries. This intention is embodied in the Constitutional provision authorizing the grant of patents, for "promoting the Progress of Science and the useful Arts."[91] That intention of disclosure further underlies many of the traditional utilitarian justifications for patents.

There is, of course, no reason that patents could not be written to be clear. The same sorts of inventions have been described in trade publications and academic journals for centuries, where clarity of explanation is prized. Instead, unclarity in patents arises out of the legal environment in which those patents are born.

For example, the claims of patents are often the most criticized parts of patents when it comes to lack of the clarity. The claims of a patent are supposed to be written "particularly pointing out and distinctly claiming" the invention,[92] so that they inform the public of what is covered by the patent and what is not.[93] However, a series of cases has whittled away at these principles, permitting even highly vague and ambiguous claims to stand valid so long as they are not "insolubly ambiguous," even if "reasonable persons will disagree" over the meaning.[94] This test fails to serve that crucial public notice function: as one patent attorney put it, "if reasonable people can disagree about the definition of the claim terms, how does this notify the public of the patentee's right to exclude?"[95] The situation is equally dismal when it comes to searching for patents of relevance to a particular company.[96] The permissibility of such unclear patents thus impedes operating businesses from safely operating, while providing no societal benefit in return.

The rules of patent interpretation sometimes encourage this unclarity. As one example, due to various court cases that have read poorly worded patent specifications as limiting the scope of patents, it is common practice to include long lists of alternatives. Consider the following definition of "electronic network" from a patent:

> Electronic Network—an electronic communication medium across which sellers and buyers may communicate, especially when communicating through the owner's main site. Representative electronic networks include the Internet, intranets, the public switched telephone network ("PSTN"), wireless voice and data networks, and television networks, such as satellite, broadcast, cable television, and two-way interac-

tive cable. Electronic networks further include hybrid systems, such as those in which sellers communicate to buyers via one medium, such as cable television, and buyers communicate to sellers via another medium, such as the Internet. Electronic networks additionally include aggregated electronic networks, such as when buyers communicate to sellers via multiple media, such the Internet, the telephone, and cable television.[97]

This definition provides no useful technical information, and is in ways contradictory to the ordinary understanding of "electronic network" (one usually does not categorize the telephone network as such), so it thus serves only to attempt to broaden the scope of the patent, at the expense of others being able to understand it easily.

More importantly, though, is the paradoxical situation that the most valuable patent is the most ambiguous patent. A patent that is prone to multiple interpretations will cost a targeted defendant more to analyze, thus making it more likely that the defendant will settle a case for a nuisance amount, and also making it more likely that any litigation over that patent will be costly and protracted. Thus, one economist traced how patents with "fuzzy boundaries" have created "a business opportunity based on acquiring patents that can be read to cover existing technologies and asserting those patents."[98] Similarly, stakeholders reported to the Federal Trade Commission that the patent system "generally creates 'an incentive to be as vague and ambiguous as you can with your claims' and to 'defer clarity at all costs.' "[99]

The patent examination process can furthermore be exploited to exacerbate patent unclarity. Often the patentability of an invention turns on the particular wording of the claims that define that invention, and the examiner's interpretation of that wording.[100] Although the examiner's interpretation ought to be set forth in writing in the record of proceedings (the "file history" or "file wrapper") for any patent,[101] in practice much of that information is never recorded.[102] Patent applicants, for example, can make oral presentations to examiners (called "interviews" in patent practice), in which the applicants explain aspects of their invention and the claims.[103] Much of this explanation is never recorded in the file history, leaving the now-owner of the patent free to assert any other interpretation of the patent that benefits the owner.[104]

Improving the clarity of the patent system is a multifaceted task, requiring support from many different areas.

4.1 Judicial Interpretations of Patent Language

Courts interpret patents during a phase of trial litigation called "claim construction,"[105] and as such have the final say in how patents are interpreted.[106] Thus, it is important that good law be issued from these courts, and especially the Federal Circuit, the court of appeals that oversees and makes many of the rules for claim construction. Among other things, courts must carefully scrutinize patents without falling victim to obfuscating techniques used to make patented inventions appear more complex, broader, or more innovative than they actually are.[107]

4.2 Patent Examination Procedures

Since the Patent Office is the first body to interpret the text of patent applications, it is critical that its reasoning be made clear and available to others wishing to understand the content of patents.

Part of this effort is simply to build a better record of the Patent Office's interpretations as it examines applications. Currently, examiners write Office Actions that identify reasons for rejecting applications, most often over prior art references. However, those Office Actions do not generally explain in detail how the examiner read the patent application or interpreted particular words in the claims.[108] Such information would benefit the public in later reading the patent, and also assist the patent applicant in understanding the basis for rejection. Furthermore, communications between the examiner and the applicant should be made of record.[109]

Additionally, the Patent Office should push for applicants to draft clearer patents. One of the requirements for granting a patent is drafted claims "particularly pointing out and distinctly claiming the subject matter which the applicant regards as his invention."[110] Patent examiners could more rigorously enforce this requirement, asking applicants to choose clearer, simpler language that more distinctly defines the invention.[111]

4.3 Limiting the Volume Game

One strategy for manufacturing unintelligibility in patents is increasing volume: applying for patents with hundreds of claims, and using continuation practice to acquire dozens of patents on the same invention.[112] This volume game contributes nothing to the public store of knowledge—an invention is secured through a few claims just as it is secured through hundreds—and the purpose of acquiring this thicket of patent claims is to increase the burden on those trying to assess the nature of the patents and operate businesses in clearance of them.[113]

Limiting this practice of unnecessary inflation of patent portfolios would contribute much to streamlining the patent system, simplifying the process for applicants, examiners, and third parties. This reform could be implemented through Patent Office rules, through legislation, and/or by judicial rule.[114]

4.4 Improved Technological Tools

Although patent language is complex and technical, it is also highly structured, potentially making it amenable to automated analysis such as natural language processing.[115] Such systems could simplify the interpretation of patents and greatly reduce the cost of having to hire experienced counsel to review patents. Additionally, automated systems would introduce a level of objectivity into patent interpretation, and potentially stave off incentives for gamesmanship in obscure patent language.

5 Targeting the Right Parties

A TRULY ASTONISHING ASPECT of the patent litigation seen today is its volume: dozens of companies sued at a time, with hundreds or thousands more the targets of demand letters. Many of the targets are not the manufacturers of supposedly infringing products, but rather the users. Thus, small businesses offering wireless Internet access have been threatened for purchasing WiFi routers,[116] iPhone application developers have been threatened for using Apple's in-app purchase mechanism,[117] and innumerable individuals and companies have been targeted simply for having a scanner in the office.[118] Today's patent wars are against end users and consumers.

5.1 Nineteenth Century Patent Trolls

Historically, this simply was not the case: patent battles, while still prevalent, were between large companies, not end users of technologies. The patent wars over sewing machines, airplanes, and automobiles, for example, involved only small numbers of patents and parties to lawsuits.[119]

In one historical case, end users of technology were targeted. During the late nineteenth century, numerous patents were granted over agrarian tools, which led to "scores of individual farmers who were sued for infringement based on farming tools they had bought, rather than invented."[120] Contemporaries at the time complained that "the country is so large and the number of articles under patent so great that there are not one-tenth of our farmers who know whether their implements are patented or not."[121] As a result, patent owners and attorneys with "'bully' and 'wily' methods often convinced the inexperienced and 'innocent' farmer that the patent covered the exact tool or implement in question and collected a royalty fee."[122] Ultimately, this led to a change in the law that made such patents much more difficult to obtain,[123] and associations of farmers also fought and won cases invalidating some of the most egregious patents, on basic farm tools like swinging gates and drivewells.[124]

Today we are seeing similar assertion of patents against end users because technology has become ubiquitous. Just as swinging gates and drivewells were necessary and widely used tools for an agrarian society in the 1800s, cell phones, computers, and software are necessary and widely used tools for every business today.

As a result, parties who ordinarily would never be involved in the patent system are being dragged into it, due to their ordinary use of software technology. The Government Accountability Office found, in a study, that 39% of patent lawsuits involving software patents were against non-technology firms:

> One representative from a retail company noted that historically, all of the patent infringement lawsuits brought against the company used to be related to products they sold. However, as of mid-2012, the representative said that half of the lawsuits against the company were related to e-commerce software that the company uses for its shopping website—such as software that allows customers to locate their stores on the website—and were brought by [patent monetization entities]. Representatives of retail and pharmaceutical companies told us they also defend lawsuits brought by PMEs related to features on their websites—typically software that outside vendors provide to them, rather than something they developed. Additionally, city public transit agencies have been sued for allegedly infringing patents by using software for real-time public transit arrival notifications, according to a few stakeholders we interviewed.[125]

These entities are attractive targets for lawsuits for a number of reasons, none of which is beneficial to the overall patent system. For one thing, end users tend to be unfamiliar with the patent system, so they are poorly equipped to defend themselves, compared to the technology companies that have dealt with such lawsuits traditionally.[126] Additionally, once end users have incorporated the manufacturer's product into their products or businesses, juries tend to unintentionally inflate the value of

A Five Part Plan for Patent Reform 25

the patent due to the unrelated features of the products or services.[127] These factors give abusive patent asserters the upper hand, without any corresponding benefit to the public or to innovation.

Finding the right solution for protecting end users is difficult. The ordinary case—a customer buys a product off the shelf and is sued for patent infringement—is straightforward and sympathetic, but there is a multitude of business arrangements between technology manufacturers and users. End users may simply use a product, may modify the product, or may incorporate it into another device. Manufacturers may make a single line of products, or multiple lines, or custom products for each customer. These and other factors demand a nuanced solution to the problem of abuses against end users of technology. Several proposed solutions are discussed below.

5.2 Redirecting Patent Suits to Manufacturers

The most direct reform would be to redirect suits against end users toward manufacturer suits in appropriate situations. Some, for example, have suggested providing immunity to patent lawsuits for end users of technology who simply purchase products off the shelf.[128] The patent owner would remain able to pursue claims against the manufacturer. This would satisfy fair compensation for the patent owner while ensuring that the patent dispute remains between parties experienced and expecting to be involved in patent lawsuits.

The difficulty with direct immunization is that there are situations in which compensation from the end user is appropriate.[129] For example, when the end user is a technology company who commissions a product from a small developer, it may be appropriate for the technology company to defend a patent infringement lawsuit. As a result, such an immunity would need to be carefully tailored with appropriate exceptions to ensure that the burden of defense is placed on the appropriate party in all situations.

One attempt to overcome this problem would be to permit lawsuits against end users but allow the manufacturer to be brought into the lawsuit as appropriate. For example, one scholar suggests an arrangement in which the end user could pull in the manufacturer into the lawsuit.[130] This relieves some pressure on the end user, since the manufacturer is now involved in the lawsuit, but it would not solve the problem of lawsuits against customers who lack the resources to even defend themselves in the first place.

5.3 Customer Suit Exception

A second option deals with the timing of lawsuits against end users, rather than the substance of the lawsuit itself. The principle, known as the "customer suit exception," is that if both the manufacturer and the end user are involved in separate patent lawsuits, then in appropriate situations the lawsuit against the end user will be "stayed," or held off, until the manufacturer suit completes.

The customer suit exception already exists in the law.[131] Courts justify the exception based on two reasons. First, if a decision is reached on the manufacturer suit, it will affect all the customer suits, but if a decision is reached on one customer suit, it will not necessarily affect other customers, so the manufacturer suit will save on overall litigation costs.[132] Second, courts recognized that, even in a suit against a customer, "in reality, the manufacturer is the true defendant in the customer suit."[133]

However, over time, courts have cut back on the customer suit exception.[134] Thus, there are several legislative proposals on the table to revive and expand the exception.[135] Doing so would help to balance the rights of patent owners and end users of products.[136]

5.4 Abolishing Software Patents Is Insufficient

A common thought is that, since many of the problems described above (and throughout this paper) arise in the field of software patents, the simple solution is to eliminate patentability of software.[137]

There are some practical issues in actually eliminating software patents (devising a definition of software patents that cannot be easily circumvented by clever lawyers is a problem[138]), but the more fundamental problem is that reforms specifically targeted toward software patents are temporary fixes for the problems of today. Although software patents are substantially problematic now,[139] this is likely because software is one of the most widely used technologies now.[140]

Analogously, as discussed above, farm technology was widely used in the nineteenth century, and patents on farm technology were hotly contested.[141] Patents on those farm tools were effectively abolished.[142] But that fix to the patent system did not prevent the software patent problems faced today—it ultimately was a Band-Aid rather than a cure.

The same would be true of eliminating software patents. The fundamental issue is that the technologies of tomorrow are unknown,[143] so targeting patent reform to one specific field of technology means that the same problems will only arise again in a different technological sector.

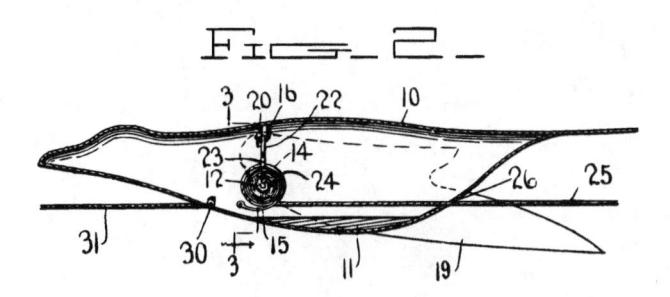

6 Avoiding Gamesmanship in Litigation

PATENTS ARE A PRIVILEGE given by the government, and as such they must be enforced through the channels of government. In the United States, this means that enforcement of patents must be through the federal district courts.[144] Thus, an essential part of the patent system must be an efficient litigation mechanism for enforcing patent rights.

However, recent history has shown a patent litigation system that is used less and less for enforcement of legitimate rights, and more and more for abusive tactics intended to enrich a few savvy litigants while impoverishing the technology-consuming public.[145] The ease of engaging in these abusive tactics, and the profitability of doing so, has given rise to an entire industry of patent litigants, known variously as non-practicing entities, patent assertion entities, or (derisively) patent trolls.[146]

Low-quality patents are often blamed for the patent troll problem.[147] And patent assertion entities often assert low-quality patents.[148] But there are numerous tactics that are entirely unrelated to the quality of the patents being asserted, tactics that drive up costs of litigation and force unjustified settlements or court awards. It is these tactics that are the subject of this section.

Abusive practices can be found through the entire patent enforcement process, from pre-litigation communications to post-trial appeals. The following are a few prominent types of abuses, and ways to address them.

6.1 Demand Letters

Prior to any lawsuit being filed, a patent owner can send a letter, arguing that the recipient of the letter infringes a patent and demanding royalty payments.[149] In itself, the process of sending a demand letter is perfectly ordinary, and even commendable insofar as it is preferable to negotiate an arrangement without having to incur the costs of court procedures.

Recently, however, a number of unscrupulous patent owners have found an easy way to abuse demand letters. They send letters to small companies, who lack the resources or experience to evaluate the merits of the arguments presented. They then are free to make outrageous or inflated claims, demanding payments without even explaining what products infringe the patents, hoping that the letter recipients are too scared or cash-strapped to fight back.

Some of these abusive demand letters even go so far as to mislead or deceive the recipients. Many threaten immediate litigation, when the sender actually has no intention of bringing a lawsuit. Some accuse recipients of infringement even when the sender has clearly not done any investigation to determine if the recipient actually infringes the patents asserted.[150] These misleading and deceptive practices have raised eyebrows, and triggered investigative efforts at both the federal and state levels.[151]

Today little is known about the world of patent demand letters, due in no small part to the efforts of the senders of those letters, who use nondisclosure agreements and shell companies to hide their activities.[152] Thus, tackling the problem of abusive demand letters must begin with learning about the scope of the demand letter economy. Proposals to create a registry of demand letters would provide that vital information, allowing lawmakers and enforcers to deal with abuses systematically.[153]

Furthermore, many of the problems with patent demand letters stem from an asymmetry between the sender, who has substantial legal resources and knowledge of the patents, and the recipient, who often lacks both. Thus, requiring certain disclosures of information in demand letters would put the recipients of those letters on more even footing.[154] That way, discussions relating to the demand letter can be based on the merits of the case, and not based on an imbalance in information.

6.2 Fair Notice to Patent Defendants

When a patent owner wishes to enforce a patent through the courts, the first step is for the patent owner to file a paper, called a complaint, with the court. The complaint should set forth the patent owner's basis for the case, and put the accused infringer on notice of what is being accused.[155]

In every other area of the law, a complaint must provide specific details about what the defendant did and how it injured the plaintiff. The defendant has a right to be put on notice of the plaintiff's arguments, so that the defendant can fairly defend the case.[156] This is called "notice pleading," and has been the law of the United States for hundreds of years.

Due to a loophole in the rules of litigation procedure, though, patent owners are currently exempt from this basic principle. A patent owner can simply name defendants and a few patent numbers on the complaint, and that is enough to get in the courtroom door.[157]

Obviously, such a bare-bones complaint fails the notice requirement and denies accused patent infringers the necessary information to mount a defense.[158] At a minimum, the accused infringer deserves to know what products are being accused, what claims of the patent are being used, and why the patent owner believes that those products infringe the patent. Thus, a simple, straightforward fix would be to require that information to be set forth in the complaint.

6.3 Costs of Litigation Procedures

Patent litigation is expensive: cases can cost millions of dollars to complete.[159] That cost can make it impossible for many small businesses to defend against even an illegitimate patent: 55% of companies sued by patent assertion entities made $10 million a year or less in revenue.[160] So the question is whether the costs of litigation can be reduced.

Part of reducing costs is limiting the volume of patent litigation, as discussed above.[161] A patent case can be expanded to be as large as the patent owner desires. The patent owner can augment the case easily:

- By accusing more products of infringement, forcing the defendant to produce volumes of documents of product development, sales and financial data, and arguments relating the additional products and the patents.

- By adding more patent claims into the lawsuit, forcing the defendant to research and interpret the additional claims, compare the accused products to those new claims, and develop new arguments.

- By obtaining additional patents from the Patent Office (through, for example, patent continuation practice), thus forcing the defendant to effectively relitigate the same case over and over again with each additional patent.

So reducing the opportunity to expand patent litigation will help to rein in costs.

A second potential area of cost reduction is in discovery, which is the portion of a lawsuit in which the parties can ask each other for documents and other information. Discovery is an essential and valuable part of our justice system, as it helps to ensure that both sides have access to truthful and complete information as they prepare their cases. But discovery can be abused, and it is often abused in patent litigation.

Abuse of the discovery process is simple: either party simply needs to demand a large number of documents or request a large volume of information. Under the current rules, the party responding to the requests has to pay for the costs of those requests, so in the face of abusive discovery that party stands to outlay enormous expenses, including time and attorney fees.

For example, a party can demand that its opponent turn over all emails relating to a certain product and dated within the last six years. In order to comply with that request, attorneys will have to gather and sift through all the emails of all the employees of a company. This typically results in a database of millions of emails. Then the attorneys will have to read through each and every one of those millions of emails, to determine which of them include information that is confidential or attorney-client privileged. As can easily be imagined, this is a time-consuming, labor-intensive, expensive process.

The simple solution to patent litigation discovery abuse is limiting discovery. Of course, care must be taken to ensure that sufficient discovery is allowed so that the case may proceed fairly and equitably. Two specific reforms, both of which have been proposed in bills introduced in Congress,[162] are directed toward alleviating discovery abuses.

First, the costs of responding to discovery can be shifted, in certain situations, to the requesting party rather than the responding party. In most patent cases, enormous volumes of documents are requested, but very few end up being used: one company reported that, in one case, 10 million documents were exchanged, but only about 2,000 were actually used at trial.[163] Making the requesting party pay for those millions of documents will incentivize the party to draw up narrower, more careful requests.

Second, the time for discovery can be shifted back to later in the litigation. Specifically, a patent case traditionally proceeds by first determining what the patent means and then determining whether the products fit within the scope of the patent. Determining what the patent means is often sufficient to determine the outcome of the case, and the meaning of the patent should generally be determinable without much discovery. Thus, the bulk of discovery could be pushed back until after the determination of the meaning of the patent.

6.4 Reasonable Royalty Computations

If a court deems a patent valid, enforceable, and infringed, then the court generally awards a "reasonable royalty" to the patent owner.[164] The reasonable royalty is intended to provide the patent owner with an appropriate fraction of the revenues earned from an infringing product; in the words of many courts, that fraction should be an amount that the patent owner and infringer would have agreed upon in a hypothetical negotiation.[165]

Simple economics dictates that the reasonable royalty should be based on the difference in value between the product with the patented feature, and the product without it (or with a noninfringing alternative).[166] Highly useful, inventive features would be more valuable to a product and thus would warrant a higher royalty; small features embedded in complex, multifunction products would warrant a lower one.[167]

Unfortunately, the methods of computing the reasonable royalty are far from simple. Courts often quote a legal test of fifteen different elements intended to help determine the reasonable royalty amount.[168] As commentators have observed, many of these fifteen factors are duplicative or unhelpful, and the sheer number of factors to consider often overwhelms the judges and juries tasked with evaluating those factors.[169] Attempts to simplify this test have not helped either: for many years a "rule of thumb" was to simply award 25% of the profits of a product, without regard to the merits of the patent at all.[170]

The complexity of assessing the reasonable royalty has led to abusive practices. For example, because one factor considered is comparable royalty rates in the industry, many patent owners put up websites or advertisements with inflated royalty rates, in hopes of influencing judges and juries to adopt those numbers. Additionally, patent owners can acquire multiple patents on the same technology, in order to inflate the apparent value of that single technology. Some patent owners will even sue a few weak targets in order to establish a "market price" for the patent.[171]

Setting the royalty rate correctly is crucial to balancing the incentives that underlie the patent system. The rate must be high enough to preserve the incentives for inventors to disclose their inventions, but too high a rate would stifle the marketplace, disincentivize further innovations, and undercut the very incentives the patent system sets out to preserve.

Determining the proper rate is a difficult task, and constructing rules to guide that determination is even more difficult. Shortcuts are not appropriate: even the 25% rule was eventually rejected for being a "fundamentally flawed tool."[172] What is certain is that the existing rules must be revised to return the reasonable royalty computation back to its basic principles, and to avoid the sort of gamesmanship that currently goes on.

6.5 Alternatives to Litigation

Given the high cost of patent litigation, one would hope for a low-cost alternative to handle some of the cases where possible. And, indeed, low-cost alternatives are provided and should be strongly supported.

The Patent Office provides several of these alternatives to litigation. Through several procedures, the Patent Office can review issued patents to determine whether those patents were validly issued or not, often in view of new information such as obscure prior art not found by the patent examiner.[173]

These Patent Office procedures have a number of advantages. For one thing, they are significantly lower in cost, because they deal with fewer issues and do not require all the trappings of court litigation.[174] Additionally, the procedures are adjudged by Patent Office employees, who generally have specialized backgrounds in technology and patent law, as opposed to judges and juries who often lack technical expertise and are confounded by the complexities of patent law.[175] Furthermore, the Patent

A Five Part Plan for Patent Reform

Office procedures facilitate early resolution of patent validity questions, because many of the procedures are open to any party who feels threatened by a patent,[176] whereas patent litigation is only available to those who have been formally sued or threatened with a specific lawsuit.[177]

Thus, the Patent Office procedures offer alternatives that potentially avoid the overbearing costs of litigation. Efforts to enlarge the use of these programs can thus further help to alleviate the potential abusive practices that arise from those overbearing costs.

Other litigation alternatives can also be envisioned. For example, some have proposed a small claims court for resolving smaller patent disputes on a lower cost basis.[178] Although ideas for a patent small claims court are generally proposed as a way to assist small patent owners, such courts could be designed to also assist small defendants, shielding those defendants from the abusive discovery practices described above, for example. Similarly, some countries provide for compulsory licensing of patents;[179] in the United States compulsory licensing is provided for certain copyrights in music[180] but not for patents.

Obviously, these litigation alternatives must be carefully considered to ensure that they provide adequate protections to both patent owners and accused infringers. But to solve the problem of skyrocketing patent litigation costs, careful consideration of alternatives is warranted.

6.6 Leveling the Playing Field

The high cost of patent litigation creates avenues for abuse, because that high cost is borne unevenly. The owner of a patent can bring lawsuits at practically no cost, while the defendant to that suit is guaranteed to have to pay enormous sums no matter what the outcome. It is this imbalance in costs, to a large degree, that has given rise to the industry of patent assertion entities, otherwise derisively termed "patent trolls."[181]

Patent assertion entities can structure their lawsuits so that they have nothing to lose when they sue others for patent infringement. Law firms will take the cases on contingency fee arrangements, so there are no legal fees to be paid. A successful plaintiff stands to win millions in court-awarded royalties—a PricewaterhouseCoopers study found a median award of $7.2 million to non-practicing entities in 2012[182]—and the unsuccessful one can just walk away. Thus, patent assertion can be a game of all upside and no downside, of no risk and all reward.

Contrast this with the dire situation of the defendant to a patent suit. Losing a case means being on the hook for millions of dollars in damages. And winning the case means being on the hook for millions of dollars in legal fees—according to the American Intellectual Property Law Association, those fees clock in between $650,000 and $5 million.[183]

The solution is to level the uneven playing field of patent law by shifting the burden of legal fees to the loser of the lawsuit. This will place appropriate responsibility on the patent owners, while giving victims of patent trolls a fighting chance against weak and questionable patents. This is why fee shifting in patent cases is part of four patent bills in Congress today.[184]

But a fee shifting law alone is no better than the paper it is printed on, because it could be easily skirted: The patent troll simply runs a business with no assets, then when attorney fees come due, it throws up its hands, declares bankruptcy, and walks away.

Thus, one proposed solution is to require a financial bond, ensuring that the plaintiff actually has the assets to pay an award of attorney fees, if necessary. Faced with an obligation to make this assurance, a patent troll with a dubious patent will think twice before aggressively overexploiting it.

Leveling the playing field of patent litigation is an important component of curbing abuses of the patent system. Those abuses will diminish when they cease to be financially viable. By undercutting the financial viability of abusive patent assertion, one would hope that those abusers would abandon the practice in favor of other, perhaps more beneficial, activities.

7 Maintaining Competition in the Innovation Economy

THE FACT THAT A PATENT is a temporary monopoly means that a patent is an exemption from the ordinary competitive free market.[185] But that fact alone does not grant the patent owner the right to engage in all manner of anticompetitive practices. As the Supreme Court has recognized, "patent and antitrust policies are both relevant in determining the 'scope of the patent monopoly.'"[186]

Nevertheless, less scrupulous patent owners have found methods of abusing the patent system to engage in anticompetitive practices that go beyond the ordinary and appropriate scope of the patent. Such anticompetitive practices include breaking of FRAND obligations and patent holdup, which are described below.

There are those who believe that, because the patent is a limited monopoly, that the patent owner ought to be authorized to use patents in any manner, regardless of the effect on competition.[187] However, this misconstrues the purpose of patents. The patent monopoly is granted not for the sake of monopoly, but as a means to technological innovation and, ultimately, a more competitive, open marketplace in technology. Thus, practices involving patents must be scrutinized, as any market practices must be scrutinized, for their effects on a competitive marketplace and consumer access to technology.[188]

7.1 FRAND Obligations

This anticompetitive problem arises with regard to so-called "standards-essential patents." These patents arise out of the technology community's use of technology standards, interoperability protocols such as WiFi or HTML, which enable different devices to communicate and operate with each other.[189] Technology standards are often adopted by bodies known as standards-setting organizations, examples of which include IEEE and ANSI.

When a company develops a new technology and wishes that technology to be incorporated into a standard, the standards-setting organization often imposes a requirement: the company must guarantee that it will fairly license any patents covering that technology.[190] This is a basic bargain: the company gets widespread adoption of its technology, in exchange for the company agreeing to lower license fees on patents to that technology.[191] This bargain is known as a "fair, reasonable and non-discriminatory," or FRAND, license obligation.[192]

The anticompetitive practice arises when a holder of a FRAND-encumbered patent breaks that obligation and begins demanding excessive royalty payments for that patent or even attempts to block sale of the product on the market.[193] Because the technology is already in a standard, other companies cannot easily move away from using that technology without breaking interoperability with other devices, thus giving the patent holder unfair leverage in the negotiations. The contractual obligation with the standards-setting organization might be avoided by transferring the patent to another party unencumbered by the obligation, a practice sometimes called "patent privateering."[194]

This behavior adversely affects the ability of companies to adopt new technologies that interoperate with other products. Interoperability is a central concern of a competitive marketplace, so the breaking of a FRAND obligation can have serious effects on competition. Additionally, it is clear that this anticompetitive practice does not further any interest in compensating the inventor, for the inventor already agreed that any royalties due under the FRAND obligation were sufficient compensation. Accordingly, reforms directed to preventing this practice are appropriate and beneficial to the technology marketplace.

7.2 Patent Holdup

Many devices today include a large number of features, any one of which could be susceptible to patenting. One study, for example, estimated that there were 250,000 patents relevant to various aspects of smartphones.[195] For such complex products and services, patents can sometimes become a "heckler's veto": any one of those 250,000 patents could block access to smartphones, particularly because a patent owner can try to obtain an injunction to block sales of a product based on even the smallest part of that product being covered a patent.[196] This problem has been described as "patent holdup," because a single patent can effectively hold up production of or access to many other unrelated technologies.[197]

A related problem is called "royalty stacking." Where royalties are awarded for individual patents, a device accused of infringing multiple patents can be subjected to multiple royalties that could theoretically reach beyond the actual profits for the device.[198] For example, if a device is found to infringe 50 patents and each of those patents is adjudged to merit a 2% royalty on revenues from the device, then 100% of the revenues of the device would go to patent licenses, meaning that the device manufacturer would have to sell the device at a loss.

Both of these problems arise out of systematic overvaluations of patents: when courts treat patents as being more valuable than they actually are, then the owners of those patents are able to forestall competition and innovation in the marketplace.[199]

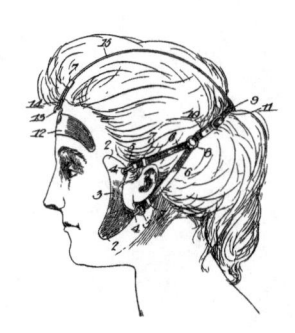

8 Conclusion: The Future of Patents

When we look back on over two hundred years of American history, we see that patents have played a central role in America's leadership in innovation. There is little question that the patent system has worked well in many respects, encouraging skilled engineers to develop new technologies and introduce those technologies to the consumer marketplace, thereby providing society with the benefits of advanced knowledge.

But just as we find that patents have often served as the seed of innovation, we also find that the patent system has served as fertile ground for the unscrupulous to take advantage of complex laws for personal benefit at the cost of societal detriment.

The future of patents will shape the future of innovation. In that future, we hope that those who invent within the patent system can work in concert with those who work outside the patent system, to maximize the innovative capacities of both groups. We hope that patents serve their intended purpose of disseminating useful knowledge and are written in clear, reasonable language that gives effective notice to all parties of what is claimed. We hope that patent holders are compensated for their inventions, not on the basis of legal manpower and litigious tactics, but on the basis of the merits of inventions and the value they contribute.

And ultimately, we hope, patents will serve as a part of a competitive and fair marketplace of technology, not geared toward transferring wealth from one party to another but rather focused on the end goal of making technology accessible and known to the consuming public. Such a patent system, then, would return to its noble roots set forth in the United States Constitution, of "promoting the Progress of Science and the useful Arts."

Appendices

A Notes

Section 1

[1] Michael Schrage, *Archaic Patent Laws Need to Be Rewritten*, L.A. TIMES, Oct. 24, 1991, at D1, *available at* http://articles.latimes.com/1991-10-24/business/fi-436_1_intellectual-property-protection.

[2] *See* Matt Levy, *Patent Progress's Guide to Patent Reform Legislation* (Nov. 19, 2013), http://www.patentprogress.org/2013/11/19/patent-progresss-guide-to-patent-reform-legislation/ (listing the bills).

[3] Joff Wild, *The Real Inventors of the Term "Patent Troll" Revealed*, INTELLECTUAL ASSET MANAGEMENT, Aug. 22, 2008, http://www.iam-magazine.com/blog/detail.aspx?g=cff2afd3-c24e-42e5-aa68-a4b4e7524177.

[4] *See* COLLEEN V. CHIEN, NEW AM. FOUND., PATENT ASSERTION AND STARTUP INNOVATION 16 & fig.3 (2013), http://www.newamerica.net/publications/policy/patent_assertion_and_startup_innovation.

[5] *See* James Bessen & Michael J. Meurer, *The Direct Costs from NPE Disputes*, 99 CORNELL L. REV. (forthcoming 2014) (manuscript at tbl.4), http://www.bu.edu/law/faculty/scholarship/workingpapers/revcov.html. The authors argue that much of that cost is deadweight loss, not contributing to compensation for inventors.

[6] *See, e.g.,* Diamond v. Chakrabarty, 447 U.S. 303, 307 (1980) ("The patent laws promote [the progress of science and the useful arts] by offering inventors exclusive rights for a limited period as an incentive for their inventiveness and research efforts."); Bonito Boats, Inc. v. Thunder Craft Boats, Inc., 489 U.S. 141, 146 (1989) ("The Patent Clause itself reflects a

balance between the need to encourage innovation and the avoidance of monopolies which stifle competition...."].

[7]*See* Mark A. Lemley, *The Myth of the Sole Inventor*, 110 MICH. L. REV. 709, 722–23, 725–26, 734–35 (2012) (noting, in many cases, that many such inventions were the result of incremental improvements made by multiple independent inventors or teams of inventors).

Section 1.1

[8]*See, e.g.,* MICHELE BOLDRIN & DAVID K. LEVINE, AGAINST INTELLECTUAL MONOPOLY 12 (2008), *available at* http://www.dklevine.com/general/intellectual/againstfinal.htm ("Since there is no evidence that intellectual monopoly achieves the desired purpose of increasing innovation and creation, it has no benefits....This leads us to our final conclusion: intellectual property is an unnecessary evil.").

[9]*See, e.g.,* Adam Mossoff, *Policy Debates on Patents Should Focus on Facts, Not Rhetoric*, FORBES, Dec. 18, 2012, http://www.forbes.com/sites/realspin/2012/12/18/policy-debates-on-patents-should-focus-on-facts-not-rhetoric/ ("Weakening intellectual property laws due to negative policy rhetoric, hyperbolic internet commentary, and extensive lobbying by firms who choose to infringe patents because they don't want to pay the licenses offered to them by patent licensing firms is irresponsible.").

Section 2.1

[10]*See* Vincenzo Denicolò & Luigi Alberto Franzoni, *The Contract Theory of Patents*, 23 INT'L REV. L. & ECON. 365, 366 (2003), *available at* http://www2.dse.unibo.it/franzoni/contract.pdf (explaining that innovation is "non-rival" in that "once it is created, it can be shared at no cost" by firms other than the inventor).

[11]*See* Jeanne C. Fromer, *Patent Disclosure*, 94 IOWA L. REV. 539, 548 (2009) ("The theory is that this stimulation occurs by rewarding inventors for taking two steps they likely would not otherwise take: to invent in the first instance and to reveal information to the public about these inventions.").

[12]*See id.* at 548–49.

[13]*See* 35 U.S.C. § 271 (2013).

[14] *See, e.g.,* Eldred v. Ashcroft, 537 U.S. 186, 225 (2003) ("The issuance of a patent is appropriately regarded as a *quid pro quo*—the grant of a limited right for the inventor's disclosure and subsequent contribution to the public domain.").

[15] *See, e.g.,* Pennock v. Dialogue, 27 U.S. (2 Pet.) 1, 19 (1829) ("While one great object was, by holding out a reasonable reward to inventors, and giving them an exclusive right to their inventions for a limited period, to stimulate the efforts of genius; the main object was 'to promote the progress of science and useful arts;' and this could be done best, by giving the public at large a right to make, construct, use, and vend the thing invented, at as early a period as possible; having a due regard to the rights of the inventor.").

[16] U.S. CONST. art. 1, § 8, cl. 8.

[17] Letter from Thomas Jefferson, to Isaac McPherson (Aug. 13, 1813), *available at* http://press-pubs.uchicago.edu/founders/documents/a1_8_8s12.html, *reprinted in* 3 THE FOUNDERS' CONSTITUTION art. 1, § 8, cl. 8, document 12 (Philip B. Kurland & Ralph Lerner eds., 1987).

Section 2.2

[18] *See* 35 U.S.C. § 112(a).

[19] *See* 35 U.S.C. § 112(b); Kirsten Osenga, *Linguistics and Patent Claim Construction*, 38 RUTGERS L.J. 61, 63–64 (2006) ("[Patent claims] must serve the dual functions of putting boundaries on the patentee's monopoly and providing sufficient notice of that monopoly to allow the public to avoid infringing the patent.").

[20] *See* U.S. PATENT & TRADEMARK OFFICE, MANUAL OF PATENT EXAMINING PROCEDURE § 2173.05(a) (8th ed., 9th rev. 2012) [hereinafter MPEP] ("Applicants...are required to make clear and precise the terms that are used to define the invention whereby the metes and bounds of the claimed invention can be ascertained.").

[21] *See* 35 U.S.C. § 102(a) (no patent should issue on an invention that "was patented, described in a printed publication, or in public use, on sale, or otherwise available to the public" before the relevant filing date); § 103 (no patent should issue if "the claimed invention as a whole would have been obvious before the effective filing date").

[22] *See* MPEP, *supra* note 20, §§ 706.02, 714. The examiner may reject the application on other grounds as well, such as indefiniteness of the claims or inadequacy of the disclosure.

[23] *See id.* § 1303.

[24] *See id.* § 1309.

[25] *See* 35 U.S.C. § 281.

[26] 35 U.S.C. § 271.

[27] *See* Markman v. Westview Instruments, Inc., 52 F.3d 967, 978–79 (Fed. Cir. 1995) (en banc), *aff'd*, 517 U.S. 370 (1996); Osenga, *supra* note 19, at 64–66; PATENT LOCAL RULES § 4 (U.S. Dist. Court for the N. Dist. of Cal. 2009), *available at* http://www.cand.uscourts.gov/localrules/patent (claim construction proceedings).

[28] 35 U.S.C. §§ 283–284.

Section 2.3

[29] *See, e.g.*, Christopher A. Harkins, *Fending Off Paper Patents and Patent Trolls: A Novel "Cold Fusion" Defense Because Changing Times Demand It*, 17 ALB. L.J. SCI. & TECH. 407, 410 (2007), *available at* http://www.brinksgilson.com/files/219.pdf (describing how a "significant cottage industry has grown up" that "ushered in the era of 'patent trolls'"). *But see* Adam Mossoff, *The Myth of the "Patent Troll" Litigation Explosion*, CENTER FOR THE PROTECTION OF INTELLECTUAL PROPERTY (Aug. 12, 2013), http://cpip.gmu.edu/2013/08/12/the-myth-of-the-patent-troll-litigation-explosion/.

[30] *See* FED. TRADE COMM'N, TO PROMOTE INNOVATION: THE PROPER BALANCE OF COMPETITION AND PATENT LAW AND POLICY ch. 2(III)(C)(2)(b)(ii)(B), at 31 (2003), *available at* http://www.ftc.gov/sites/default/files/documents/reports/promote-innovation-proper-balance-competition-and-patent-law-and-policy/innovationrpt.pdf (describing characteristics of NPEs); Colleen V. Chien, *From Arms Race to Marketplace: The Complex Patent Ecosystem and Its Implications for the Patent System*, 62 HASTINGS L.J. 297, 328 (2010), *available at* http://www.hastingslawjournal.org/wp-content/uploads/2011/02/Chien_62-HLJ-297.pdf ("Patent-assertion entities are focused on the enforcement, rather than the active development or commercialization of their patents."); Sara Jeruss et al., *The America Invents Act 500: Effects of Patent Monetization Entities on US Litigation*,

11 DUKE L. & TECH. REV. 357, 370 (2012), *available at* http://scholarship. law.duke.edu/dltr/vol11/iss2/6/ (defining patent monetization entities as ones that "described their main source of revenue as patent litigation or licensing").

[31] *See* John F. Duffy, *Reviving the Paper Patent Doctrine*, 98 CORNELL L. REV. 1359, 1395 (2013), *available at* http://cornelllawreview.org/files/ 2013/10/98CLR1359.pdf ("Holding all else equal, a practiced patent discloses more, teaches more, and contributes more to the sum total of social knowledge than does a mere paper patent.").

[32] *See* Mark A. Lemley & Douglas Melamed, *Missing the Forest for the Trolls*, 113 COLUM. L. REV. 2117, 2165 (2013), *available at* http:// columbialawreview.org/missing-the-forest-for-the-trolls-3/ ("It seems likely that practicing entities have in the past been more concerned than trolls about such reputational matters.").

[33] *See id.* at 2170 ("When it comes to patent enforcement, it is hard to conclude that trolls cost society more than practicing entities.").

Section 3

[34] *See, e.g.,* Fromer, *supra* note 11, at 547 & n.31 (citing sources).

[35] *See* Rebecca S. Eisenberg, *The Role of the FDA in Innovation Policy*, 13 MICH. TELECOMM. & TECH. L. REV. 345, 350 (2007), *available at* http:// www.mttlr.org/volthirteen/eisenberg.pdf ("Biopharmaceutical research is often held out as a shining example of the success of the patent system in motivating private investment in R&D.").

[36] *See id.* at 346 (noting that patent advocates cite drug regulation "as a large part of the cost of drug development that can only be recovered if firms are allowed to charge patent-protected premium prices for new products."). *But see id.* at 359 (arguing that FDA regulation of new drugs in fact acts as a "pseudo-patent" complementing patent exclusivity).

[37] *See, e.g.,* Wendy Seltzer, *Software Patents and/or Software Development*, 78 BROOKLYN L. REV. 929, 929 (2013), *available at* http:// www.brooklaw.edu/~/media/PDF/LawJournals/BLR_PDF/blr_v78iii.ashx ("Patents do not provide a useful incentive to innovate in the software industry, I contend, because the patent promise ill-suits the engineering and development practices and business strategies of software production."); Lemley, *supra* note 7, at 736–38; Brief of *Amici Curiae* Check-

point Software, Inc., et al., in Support of Respondents at 3, Alice Corp. Pty. Ltd. v. CLS Bank Int'l, No. 13-298 (U.S. Feb. 27, 2014), *available at* http://www.americanbar.org/content/dam/aba/publications/supreme_court_preview/briefs-v3/13-298_resp_amcu_cs-etal.pdf ("Software patents are not necessary to spur innovation among the Amici. Our engineers do not innovate because they hope to get patents.").

[38]*See* Kewanee Oil Co. v. Bicron Corp., 416 U.S. 470, 484 (1974) ("Certainly the patent policy of encouraging invention is not disturbed by the existence of another form of incentive to invention.").

Section 3.1

[39] ANDREAS PAPPAS, VISIONMOBILE LTD., APP ECONOMY FORECASTS 2013–2016 (2013).

[40] MICHAEL MANDEL, WHERE THE JOBS ARE: THE APP ECONOMY 13 (2012).

[41]*See* Peter S. Menell, *Indirect Copyright Liability and Technological Innovation*, 32 COLUM. J.L. & ARTS 375, 389 (2009) ("Many of the notable innovations—from Napster's peer-to-peer system to the Google search engine, YouTube, and Facebook—were hatched and initially developed in the Web 2.0 equivalent of the Silicon Valley garage: a dorm room."); Seltzer, *supra* note 37, at 973 (noting that the software industry features "lower capital costs…; lower pure research costs and a focus on implementation; and lower uncertainty of development").

[42] Mark A. Lemley, *Reconceiving Patents in the Age of Venture Capital*, 4 J. SMALL & EMERGING BUS. L. 137, 138 n.3 (2000) (citing that cost as "not unreasonable based on my experience"); *see also* Gene Quinn, *The Cost of Obtaining a Patent in the US*, IPWATCHDOG (Jan. 28, 2011), http://www.ipwatchdog.com/2011/01/28/the-cost-of-obtaining-patent/ (citing costs of $5,000 to $15,000 for filing the application alone).

[43] The startup accelerator Y Combinator, for example, invests $20,000 for a three-person startup. *See* Steven Levy, *Y Combinator Is Boot Camp for Startups*, WIRED (May 17, 2011), http://www.wired.com/magazine/2011/05/ff_ycombinator/.

[44] Seltzer, *supra* note 37, at 982–83.

[45]*Id.* at 983–84.

[46] *See* ERIC RIES, THE LEAN STARTUP: HOW TODAY'S ENTREPRENEURS USE CONTINUOUS INNOVATION TO CREATE RADICALLY SUCCESSFUL BUSINESSES 149 (2011) (describing a pivot as "a structured course correction designed to test a new fundamental hypothesis about the product, strategy, and engine of growth").

Section 3.2

[47] The term "open innovation community" is from Jason Schultz & Jennifer M. Urban, *Protecting Open Innovation: The Defensive Patent License as a New Approach to Patent Threats, Transaction Costs, and Tactical Disarmament*, 26 HARV. J.L. & TECH. 1, 2 n.1 (2012), *available at* http://jolt.law.harvard.edu/articles/pdf/v26/26HarvJLTech1.pdf.

[48] *See id.* at 2 & n.1.

[49] ERIC S. RAYMOND, THE CATHEDRAL AND THE BAZAAR: MUSINGS ON LINUX AND OPEN SOURCE BY AN ACCIDENTAL REVOLUTIONARY 43 (rev. ed. 2001) (describing Linux and fetchmail); *see also* Schultz & Urban, *supra* note 47, at 17.

[50] *See* YOCHAI BENKLER, THE WEALTH OF NETWORKS: HOW SOCIAL PRODUCTION TRANSFORMS MARKETS AND FREEDOM 46 (2006), *available at* http://www.benkler.org/Benkler_Wealth_Of_Networks.pdf; Jon Brodkin, *How Red Hat Killed Its Core Product—And Became a Billion-Dollar Business*, ARS TECHNICA, Feb. 28, 2012, http://arstechnica.com/business/2012/02/how-red-hat-killed-its-core-productand-became-a-billion-dollar-business/.

[51] *See, e.g.*, RICHARD M. STALLMAN, FREE SOFTWARE, FREE SOCIETY 129 (2d ed. 2010), *available at* http://www.gnu.org/doc/fsfs-ii-2.pdf ("My work on free software is motivated by an idealistic goal: spreading freedom and cooperation. I want to encourage free software to spread, replacing proprietary software that forbids cooperation, and thus make our society better.").

Section 3.3

[52] Joseph Stiglitz, *Give Prizes Not Patents*, NEW SCIENTIST, Sept. 16, 2006, at 21, *available at* http://www2.gsb.columbia.edu/faculty/jstiglitz/download/2006_New_Scientist.pdf; *see also* Michael Kremer, *Patent Buyouts: A Mechanism for Encouraging Innovation*, 113 THE QUARTERLY JOUR-

NAL OF ECONOMICS 1137 (1998) (proposing an auction process by which the government buys out most patents, offering the buyout price as a prize).

[53] Alfred Bernhard Nobel, *Alfred Nobel's Will* (Nov. 27, 1895), http://www.nobelprize.org/alfred_nobel/will/will-full.html.

[54] For a comprehensive overview of rewards for innovation, see generally Daniel J. Hemel & Lisa Larrimore Ouellette, *Beyond the Patents—Prizes Debate*, 92 TEX. L. REV. 304 (2013), *available at* http://www.texaslrev.com/wp-content/uploads/HemelOuellette.pdf.

[55] Much of early Internet technology research was funded by the Advanced Research Projects Agency (ARPA, now DARPA). *See* ROBERT H. ZAKON, REQUEST FOR COMMENTS 2235: HOBBES' INTERNET TIMELINE 1–6 (1997), http://tools.ietf.org/html/rfc2235.

[56] 35 U.S.C. §§ 200–212 (2013).

[57] More specifically, if a participant in a W3C standard acquires a patent essential to the standard, the participant must generally grant a royalty-free license to the public for that patent. Daniel J. Weitzner, *W3C Patent Policy*, W3.ORG §§ 3.1, 5 (Feb. 5, 2004), http://www.w3.org/Consortium/Patent-Policy-20040205/.

Section 3.4

[58] *See, e.g.*, CHIEN, *supra* note 4, at 16–17 & fig.3; *When Patents Attack!*, THIS AMERICAN LIFE 6:20–37 (July 22, 2011), http://www.thisamericanlife.org/radio-archives/episode/441/when-patents-attack ("[Interviewer]: Did it put your business in danger? [Startup founder] Jeff Kelling: It did, and they knew that. The settlement they wanted to get was just enough to put us in danger, but not to close us, and I'll stop there.").

[59] Press Release, Karen Duffin, Bite Commc'ns for OSRM, *Results of First-Ever Linux Patent Review Announced, Patent Insurance Offered by Open Source Risk Management* 1 (Aug. 2, 2004), http://www.osriskmanagement.com/press_releases/press_release_080204.pdf.

[60] Press Release, Dep't of Justice, *CPTN Holdings LLC and Novell Inc. Change Deal in Order to Address Department of Justice's Open Source Concerns* (Apr. 20, 2011), *available at* http://www.justice.gov/opa/pr/2011/April/11-at-491.html.

[61] Richard Stallman, *Why Upgrade to GPLv3* (July 29, 2013), https://www.gnu.org/licenses/rms-why-gplv3.html; *The GNU General Public License v.3.0* § 11 (June 29, 2007), http://www.gnu.org/licenses/gpl.html.

[62] *See* Whittemore v. Cutter, 29 F. Cas. 1120, 1121 (C.C.D. Mass. 1813) ("[I]t could never have been the intention of the legislature to punish a man, who constructed such a machine merely for philosophical experiments."); *In re* Rosuvastatin Calcium Patent Litig., 703 F.3d 511, 527 (Fed. Cir. 2012) ("However, patenting does not deprive the public of the right to experiment with and improve upon the patented subject matter."); *see also* CLS Bank Int'l v. Alice Corp., 717 F.3d 1269, 1322–25 (Fed. Cir. 2013) (en banc) (Newman, J., concurring and dissenting) (discussing experimental use doctrine), *cert. granted*, 134 S. Ct. 734 (2013).

[63] *See* Rebecca S. Eisenberg, *Patents and the Progress of Science: Exclusive Rights and Experimental Use*, 56 U. CHI. L. REV. 1017, 1019–20 (1989) ("For the most part, the courts have held that the experimental use defense does not apply to the facts of the particular cases before them.").

Section 3.5

[64] *See* discussion *supra* note 62 and accompanying text.

[65] Schultz & Urban, *supra* note 47, at 38–39.

[66] *Id.* at 38.

[67] For another example of such an alternate patent license, see Adam Messinger, *Introducing the Innovator's Patent Agreement*, THE OFFICIAL TWITTER BLOG (Apr. 17, 2012), https://blog.twitter.com/2012/introducing-innovators-patent-agreement.

Section 3.6

[68] *See, e.g.*, FED. TRADE COMM'N, *supra* note 30, at ch. 4(II)(A)(3), at 8 ("Several participants voiced concern about too great an issuance of obvious patents.").

[69] *See, e.g.*, Press Release, Elec. Frontier Found., *EFF Files Challenge with Patent Office Against Troll's Podcasting Patent* (Oct. 16, 2013), https://www.eff.org/press/releases/eff-files-challenge-patent-office-against-trolls-podcasting-patent.

[70] *See generally* Sara-Jayne Adams, *Quality Is the Key to a Bright Patent Future*, INTELL. ASSET MGMT., Apr./May 2008, at 55, *available at* http://www.iam-magazine.com/Issues/Article.ashx?g=7ec06ce7-8c64-4402-9222-f79e3aaaf171 (collecting numerous views on patent quality).

[71] "The world goes ahead because each of us builds on the work of our predecessors. 'A dwarf standing on the shoulders of a giant can see farther than the giant himself.' " Sony Corp. of Am. v. Universal City Studios, Inc., 464 U.S. 417, 477 n.28 (1984) (quoting Zechariah Chafee, Jr., *Reflections on the Law of Copyright: I*, 45 COLUM. L. REV. 503, 511 (1945)); *see also* Lemley, *supra* note 7, at 714; Letter from Isaac Newton, to Robert Hooke (Feb. 5, 1675), *available at* http://digitallibrary.hsp.org/index.php/Detail/Object/Show/object_id/9565 ("If I have seen further it is by standing on the shoulders [*sic*] of Giants.").

[72] Bilski v. Kappos, 130 S. Ct. 3218, 3225 (2010) (quoting Funk Bros. Seed Co. v. Kalo Inoculant Co., 333 U.S. 127, 130 (1948)) (omission in original).

[73] *See* 35 U.S.C. § 102 (2013).

[74] 35 U.S.C. § 103.

[75] *See* Great Atl. & Pac. Tea Co. v. Supermarket Equip. Corp., 340 U.S. 147, 152–53 (1950) (an obvious patent "withdraws what already is known into the field of its monopoly and diminishes the resources available to skillful men").

[76] *See* MPEP, *supra* note 20, § 902.03(e); Beth Simone Noveck, *"Peer to Patent": Collective Intelligence, Open Review, and Patent Reform*, 20 HARV. J.L. & TECH. 123, 135 (2006).

[77] There have been several formal efforts toward externalizing, or "crowdsourcing," the prior art review effort. *See* Press Release, Peter Pappas, U.S. Patent & Trademark Office, *USPTO Launches Second Peer To Patent Pilot in Collaboration with New York Law School* (Oct. 19, 2010), http://www.uspto.gov/news/pr/2010/10_50.jsp; 35 U.S.C. § 122(e)(1) (preissuance submissions by third parties in pending patent applications); Press Release, Office of the Press Sec'y, The White House, *Fact Sheet—Executive Actions: Answering the President's Call to Strengthen Our Patent System and Foster Innovation* (Feb. 20, 2014) [hereinafter White House Executive Actions], http://www.whitehouse.gov/the-press-office/2014/02/20/fact-sheet-executive-actions-answering-president-s-call-strengthen-

our-p ("[T]he USPTO is announcing a new initiative focused on expanding ways for companies, experts, and the general public to help patent examiners, holders, and applicants find relevant 'prior art'....")

[78] KSR Int'l Co. v. Teleflex Inc., 550 U.S. 398 (2007).

[79] *Id.* at 1734.

[80] *Id.* at 1742.

[81] *See, e.g.,* Kinetic Concepts, Inc. v. Smith & Nephew, Inc., 688 F.3d 1342, 1368–69 (Fed. Cir. 2012) (reversing a finding of obviousness for a patent due in part to a lack of expert testimony on motivation to combine).

[82] *See* Charles Duan, Pub. Knowledge, *Comments of Public Knowledge, the Electronic Frontier Foundation, and Engine Advocacy on Prior Art Resources for Use in the Examination of Software-Related Patent Applications* 4–6 (Mar. 17, 2014), *available at* https://www.eff.org/files/2014/03/17/comments_to_pto_from_public_knowledge_eff_engine.pdf.

[83] *See, e.g.,* Request for Comments and Notice of Roundtable Event on the Use of Crowdsourcing and Third-Party Preissuance Submissions to Identify Relevant Prior Art, 79 Fed. Reg. 15,319 (U.S. Patent & Trademark Office 2014).

Section 4

[84] This section is drawn in part from Brief of Public Knowledge and the Electronic Frontier Foundation as *Amici Curiae* in Support of Petitioner, Nautilus, Inc. v. Biosig Instruments, Inc., No. 13-369 (U.S. Oct. 23, 2013).

[85] Lisa Larrimore Ouellette, *Do Patents Disclose Useful Information?*, 25 HARV. J.L. & TECH. 545 (2012).

[86] *Id.* at 571.

[87] *Id.* at 576.

[88] *Id.*

[89] Rob Weir, *How Not to Read a Patent* (Aug. 13, 2009), http://www.robweir.com/blog/2009/08/how-not-to-read-patent.html.

[90] Rich Steeves, *New Report Examines the Economic Cost of Patent Trolls*, INSIDECOUNSEL (Oct. 11, 2013), http://www.insidecounsel.com/2013/10/11/new-report-examines-the-economic-cost-of-patent-tr.

[91] U.S. CONST. art. 1, § 8, cl. 8.

[92] 35 U.S.C. § 112(b) (2013).

[93] *See* McClain v. Ortmayer, 141 U.S. 419, 424 (1891) (holding that a patent claim secures "all to which [the patentee] is entitled" while "appris[ing] the public of what is still open to them"); United Carbon Co. v. Binney & Smith Co., 317 U.S. 228, 236 (1942) (finding that ambiguous patent claims create a "zone of uncertainty" that will "discourage invention"); Gen. Elec. Corp. v. Wabash Appliance Corp., 304 U.S. 364, 369 (1938) ("The limits of a patent must be known for...the assurance that the subject of the patent will be dedicated ultimately to the public.").

[94] Exxon Research & Eng'g Co. v. United States, 265 F.3d 1371, 1375 (Fed. Cir. 2001); *accord* Datamize, LLC v. Plumtree Software, Inc., 417 F.3d 1342, 1437 (Fed. Cir. 2005).

[95] Kirk M. Hartung, *Claim Construction: Another Matter of Chance and Confusion*, 88 J. PAT. & TRADEMARK OFF. SOC'Y 831, 844 (2006); *see also* Christa J. Laser, *A Definite Claim On Claim Indefiniteness*, 10 CHI.-KENT J. INTELL. PROP. 25, 27 (2010) ("If the Federal Circuit does not correct this trend soon, a competitor's ability to accurately determine the metes and bounds of current patents might deteriorate further."); Lemley, *supra* note 7, at 745 ("[T]he Federal Circuit has permitted a number of vague general disclosures that don't actually communicate very much to anyone, and patent lawyers often have incentives to write such vague disclosures.").

[96] Christina Mulligan & Timothy B. Lee, *Scaling the Patent System*, 68 N.Y.U. ANN. SURV. AM. L. 289, 297–98 (2012).

[97] U.S. Patent No. 7,480,627 col. 4, ll. 26–40 (filed Oct. 10, 2000).

[98] James Bessen et al., *The Private and Social Costs of Patent Trolls*, REGULATION, Winter 2011–2012, at 26, 34, http://object.cato.org/sites/cato.org/files/serials/files/regulation/2012/5/v34n4-1.pdf.

[99] FED. TRADE COMM'N, THE EVOLVING IP MARKETPLACE: ALIGNING PATENT NOTICE AND REMEDIES WITH COMPETITION 85 (2011); *see also* PHIL GOLDBERG, PROGRESSIVE POLICY INST., STUMPING PATENT TROLLS ON THE BRIDGE TO INNOVATION 3 (2013) (citing "vague or expansive terms" in patents as one of "three cross winds" creating a flood of patent litigation); David Segal, *Has Patent, Will Sue: An Alert to Corporate America*, N.Y. TIMES, July 14, 2013, at BU1 ("But as long as the [patent] system exists, [noted patent

assertor Erich] Spangenberg is going to exploit its ambiguities and pokiness for all it's worth."); JAMES BESSEN & MICHAEL J. MEURER, PATENT FAILURE: HOW JUDGES, BUREAUCRATS, AND LAWYERS PUT INNOVATORS AT RISK 164 (2008) ("The evidence suggests . . . that the deterioration of the notice function might be the central factor fueling the growth in patent litigation").

[100] *See* Phillips v. AWH Corp., 415 F.3d 1303, 1317 (Fed. Cir. 2005) ("[T]he prosecution history provides evidence of how the PTO and the inventor understood the patent." (citing Lemelson v. Gen. Mills, Inc., 968 F.2d 1202, 1206 (Fed. Cir. 1992))).

[101] *See* 37 C.F.R. § 1.2 (2013) ("All business with the Patent and Trademark Office should be transacted in writing."); 37 C.F.R. § 1.133(b) (2013) ("In every instance where reconsideration is requested in view of an interview with an examiner, a complete written statement of the reasons presented at the interview as warranting favorable action must be filed by the applicant.").

[102] *See Phillips*, 415 F.3d at 1317 (observing that the file wrapper is "less useful for claim construction purposes" because it "often lacks the clarity of the specification").

[103] *See* 37 C.F.R. § 1.133; MPEP, *supra* note 20, § 713.

[104] Elec. Frontier Found., *Comments of EFF on Enhancement of Quality of Software-Related Patents* 12 (Apr. 15, 2013), *available at* https://www.eff.org/files/eff_comments_on_enhancement_of_quality_of_software-related_patents.pdf ("Summaries [of interviews] are often too vague and brief to provide meaningful notice to the public. The lack of a full record means that applicants can make arguments in interviews without facing the estoppel issues that would accompany a written filing."); *see also* Susan Lynch, *Interviewing Patent Examiners—Advantageous or Disastrous?* (Feb. 15, 2006), http://www.ipfrontline.com/depts/article.aspx?id=721&deptid=4 ("Another possible reason to argue the merits of a patent application orally rather than in writing is to avoid placing statements in the record that can be used against a patentee years later…. Although the USPTO rules require patent applicants to provide a written record of an interview to be placed into the application file, statements in such written records are much more limited."); Matthew R. Osenga, *Interviews with Patent Examiners* (Apr. 30, 2012), http://inventivestep.net/2012/04/30/interviews-with-patent-examiners/ (patent attorney noting

that, for some arguments presented in an interview, "I may omit it from my next response, thereby keeping it out of the record"); *cf.* MPEP, *supra* note 20, § 713.04 ("A complete written statement as to the substance of any face-to-face, video conference, electronic mail or telephone interview with regard to the merits of an application must be made of record in the application, whether or not an agreement with the examiner was reached at the interview.").

Section 4.1

[105] *See, e.g.*, N. DIST. OF CAL. PATENT LOCAL RULES §§ 4-1 to -7 (2009), *available at* http://www.cand.uscourts.gov/localrules/patent.

[106] *See* Markman v. Westview Instruments, Inc., 517 U.S. 370, 391 (1996) (holding that interpretation of claim terms is "an issue for the judge, not the jury"); Cybor Corp. v. FAS Techs., Inc., 138 F.3d 1448, 1456 (Fed. Cir. 1998) ("[A]s a purely legal question, we review claim construction de novo on appeal including any allegedly fact-based questions relating to claim construction.").

[107] For an example of this situation, see Brief of *Amicus Curiae* Public Knowledge in Support of Petitioner, WildTangent, Inc. v. Ultramercial, LLC, No. 13-255 (June 21, 2013), *available at* http://www.publicknowledge.org/files/wildtangent-v-ultramercial-pk-amicus.pdf.

Section 4.2

[108] *See* Phillips v. AWH Corp., 415 F.3d 1303, 1317 (Fed. Cir. 2005) (noting that an Office Action "often lacks the clarity of the specification and thus is less useful for claim construction purposes").

[109] *See* Charles Duan, *Comments of Public Knowledge and the Electronic Frontier Foundation on the United States Patent and Trademark Office Software Partnership Meeting* 4 (Oct. 24, 2013), http://www.uspto.gov/patents/init_events/swglossary_a_eff_2013oct24.pdf.

[110] 35 U.S.C. § 112(b) (2013).

[111] The Patent Office is currently looking at a "pilot program aimed at encouraging the use of clearer language within patent claims." White House Executive Actions, *supra* note 77.

Section 4.3

[112] *See* Mark A. Lemley & Kimberly A. Moore, *Ending Abuse of Patent Continuations*, 84 B.U. L. REV. 63, 81 (2004).

[113] *See* Carl Shapiro, *Navigating the Patent Thicket: Cross Licenses, Patent Pools, and Standard Setting*, in 1 INNOVATION POLICY AND THE ECONOMY 119, 126 (Adam B. Jaffe et al. eds., 2001) ("In short, with multiple overlapping patents...we have a volatile mix of two powerful types of transaction costs that can burden innovation...."); Lemley & Moore, *supra* note 112, at 82–83 (noting particularly that such continuation practice with respect to pharmaceutical patents "serves no useful social purpose").

[114] The USPTO attempted to institute certain limiting rules on continuations, but that effort was rejected by the Federal Circuit, *see* Tafas v. Doll, 559 F.3d 1345 (Fed. Cir. 2009), and the USPTO declined to pursue the effort further, instead voluntarily rescinding the proposed rules, *see* Tafas v. Kappos, 586 F.3d 1369 (Fed. Cir. 2009).

Section 4.4

[115] *See, e.g.,* Svetlana Sheremetyeva, *Natural Language Analysis of Patent Claims*, 20 PROC. ACL-2003 WORKSHOP ON PAT. CORPUS PROCESSING 66 (2003), *available at* http://acl.ldc.upenn.edu/W/W03/W03-2008.pdf.

Section 5

[116] John Ribeiro, *Cisco Reaches Agreement with Innovatio over Wi-Fi Patents*, PCWORLD (Feb. 7, 2014), http://www.pcworld.com/article/2095700/cisco-reaches-agreement-with-innovatio-over-wifi-patents.html.

[117] Erik Slivka, *Lodsys Threatens to Sue App Store Developers Over In-App Purchases and Upgrade Links*, MACRUMORS (May 13, 2011), http://www.macrumors.com/2011/05/13/lodsys-threatens-to-sue-app-store-developers-over-purchase-links/.

[118] Joe Mullin, *Patent Trolls Want $1,000—for Using Scanners*, ARS TECHNICA (Jan. 2, 2013), http://arstechnica.com/tech-policy/2013/01/patent-trolls-want-1000-for-using-scanners/.

Section 5.1

[119] *See* Colleen V. Chien, *Reforming Software Patents*, 50 Hous. L. Rev. 325, 336–37 (2012), *available at* http://www.houstonlawreview.org/wp-content/uploads/2013/02/2-Chien.pdf.

[120] *Id.* at 330.

[121] Earl W. Hayter, *The Patent System and Agrarian Discontent, 1875-1888*, 34 Miss. Valley Hist. Rev. 59, 65 (1947).

[122] *Id.* at 66.

[123] *See* Chien, *supra* note 119, at 348.

[124] *See* Hayter, *supra* note 121, at 73–74, 76–77.

[125] U.S. Gov't Accountability Office, GAO-13-465, Intellectual Property: Assessing Factors that Affect Patent Infringement Litigation Could Help Improve Patent Quality 23 (2013), *available at* http://www.gao.gov/assets/660/657103.pdf.

[126] *See* Brian J. Love & James C. Yoon, *Expanding Patent Law's Customer Suit Exception*, 93 B.U. L. Rev. 1605, 1614 (2013), *available at* http://www.bu.edu/bulawreview/files/2013/10/LOVE-YOON_Expanding-Patent.pdf ("Also, compared to customers, manufacturers have a relative advantage litigating patent suits because they generally have greater knowledge of the industry, the prior art, and the patented invention's value.").

[127] *See id.* at 1633–34 ("[T]he larger the accused device, the harder it is for jurors to distinguish between value attributable to the patented invention and value attributable to other features and components."); Bernard Chao, *The Case for Contribution in Patent Law*, 80 U. Cin. L. Rev. 113, 122 (2011), http://scholarship.law.uc.edu/cgi/viewcontent.cgi?article=1083&context=uclr (discussing the "overcompensation problem" that is "particularly true when the patent involved only covers a single component of a multiple component product").

Section 5.2

[128] David Long & Matt Rizzolo, *Protecting "End Users" from Patent Infringement Actions*, InsideCounsel (Sept. 18, 2013), http://www.insidecounsel.com/2013/09/18/protecting-end-users-from-patent-infringement-acti (citing the Electronic Frontier Foundation's statement on

legislative solutions for patent reform); Alan Schoenbaum, *Immunize End Users from Patent Trolls*, RACKSPACE BLOG (Mar. 19, 2013), http://www.rackspace.com/blog/immunize-end-users-from-patent-trolls/ ("Congressman Farenthold offered a simple, workable solution to solve a big part of the problem: immunize end users of commodity-type products from patent litigation.").

[129] *See, e.g.,* Dennis Crouch, *Capturing the Consumer Surplus Through Downstream Licensing and Infringement Lawsuits*, PATENTLY-O (Dec. 6, 2013), http://patentlyo.com/patent/2013/12/capturing-the-consumer-surplus-through-downstream-licensing-and-infringement-lawsuits.html (suggesting an economic model in which theoretically compensation from an end user would be appropriate). *But see id.* (noting that, in reality, the aforementioned analysis, "even if mathematically correct, is largely irrelevant in the current climate").

[130] *See* Chao, *supra* note 127, at 132–34. Chao adopts theory of contributory liability from torts, under which, if two people cause an injury and one of those two is sued, the sued person can bring in the other person. "If contribution were applied to patent law, manufacturers of multi-component products accused of patent infringement would be able to demand that any supplier of an infringing component share in any potential liability." *Id.* at 133.

Section 5.3

[131] Katz v. Lear Siegler, Inc., 909 F.2d 1459, 1464 (Fed. Cir. 1990) (explaining that, under the customer suit exception, "litigation against or brought by the manufacturer of infringing goods takes precedence over a suit by the patent owner against customers of the manufacturer").

[132] *See* Love & Yoon, *supra* note 126, at 1616–17 ("In its first few decades of existence, courts applied the customer suit exception relatively liberally, justifying its application on efficiency grounds....").

[133] *See* Codex Corp. v. Milgo Elec. Corp., 553 F.2d 735, 737–38 (1st Cir. 1977); Love & Yoon, *supra* note 126, at 1617.

[134] *See* Love & Yoon, *supra* note 126, at 1617–18.

[135] *See* Innovation Act, H.R. 3309, 113th Cong. sec. 5, § 296 (as referred to Senate, Dec. 9, 2013); Patent Transparency and Improvements Act, S.

1720, 113th Cong. sec. 4, § 299A (2013); Patent Litigation and Innovation Act, H.R. 2639, 113th Cong. sec. 4, § 300 (2013).

[136] Love & Yoon, *supra* note 126, at 1635.

Section 5.4

[137] *See, e.g.,* Timothy B. Lee, *The Supreme Court Could Abolish Software Patents Next Year. Here's Why It Should*, WASHINGTON POST: THE SWITCH (Dec. 6, 2013), http://www.washingtonpost.com/blogs/the-switch/wp/2013/12/06/the-supreme-court-could-abolish-software-patents-next-year-heres-why-it-should/ ("Reiterating that "pure" software can't be patented wouldn't just be good law — it would also save the nation billions of dollars in litigation costs."); David A. Burton, *Software Developers Want Changes in Patent and Copyright Law*, 3 MICH. TELECOMM. & TECH. L. REV. 87, 88–90 (1996), http://www.mttlr.org/voltwo/burton.pdf (finding, in an informal survey of 49 software programmers, that 29 of them (59%) thought that the United States should abolish software patents).

[138] *See* Chien, *supra* note 119, at 354 (" One of the biggest challenges to 'abolishing software patents' is the question of what exactly is a 'software patent'?"). *But see id.* at 356 (suggesting that "a working definition, rather than a perfect definition, may be what is really needed").

[139] *See, e.g.,* U.S. GOV'T ACCOUNTABILITY OFFICE, *supra* note 125, at 22 ("Specifically, about 84 percent of [patent monetization entity] lawsuits from 2007 to 2011 involved software-related patents...."); James Bessen, *The Patent Troll Crisis Is Really a Software Patent Crisis*, WASHINGTON POST: THE SWITCH (Sept. 3, 2013), http://www.washingtonpost.com/blogs/the-switch/wp/2013/09/03/the-patent-troll-crisis-is-really-a-software-patent-crisis/.

[140] *See, e.g.,* ERIK BRYNJOLFSSON & ADAM SAUNDERS, WIRED FOR INNOVATION: HOW INFORMATION TECHNOLOGY IS RESHAPING THE ECONOMY 10 (2010) ("The difference between being a winner and being a lagging firm in IT-intensive industries is very large and growing. Using technology effectively matters more now than ever before.").

[141] *See* Section 5.1 *supra* p. 23.

[142] *See* Chien, *supra* note 119, at 348.

[143] As an example, as the 3D printing industry grows, so does interest in patents on 3D printing. *See, e.g.,* Heesun Wee, *The "Gold Rush" for 3-*

D Printing Patents (Aug. 15, 2013), http://www.cnbc.com/id/100942655, CNBC.com (describing the "patent land grab of 3-D intellectual property").

Section 6

[144] *See* 35 U.S.C. § 281 (2013).

[145] *See, e.g.,* GOLDBERG, *supra* note 99, at 5 ("By filing plausible claims raising sufficient risk of loss for defendants, [PAEs] force companies to choose between expending millions of dollars to litigate the claims or settle for less than the cost of the litigation….[M]ost patent assertions are meant to drive settlements.").

[146] *See* FED. TRADE COMM'N, *supra* note 99, at 50 nn.2 & 60 (distinguishing these terms).

[147] *See, e.g.,* U.S. GOV'T ACCOUNTABILITY OFFICE, *supra* note 125, at 31–32 ("Some of the representatives from operating companies also said that [patent monetizing entities] are often more willing to bring lawsuits based on a broad interpretation of their patents' claims…."); Erin Mershon, *White House Aims to Undercut Patent Trolls*, POLITICO (Feb. 20, 2014), http://www.politico.com/story/2014/02/white-house-rolls-out-patent-actions-103727.html ("Critics say patent trolls amass vague or low-quality patents and use them to sue or extract licensing fees from companies, putting a strain on businesses and the larger economy.").

[148] As one study found, nonpracticing entities owned 63.5% of the most-litigated patents. John R. Allison et al., *Patent Quality and Settlement Among Repeat Patent Litigants*, 99 GEO. L.J. 677, 708 (2011), *available at* http://georgetownlawjournal.org/files/pdf/99-3/AllisonLemleyWalker%2520677-712.PDF. The study further found that NPEs won only 8% of their cases on the merits, while operating companies won 40% of their cases. *Id.*

Section 6.1

[149] *See, e.g.,* Stephen Wang, *The Impact of Patent Troll Demand Letters*, PUBLIC KNOWLEDGE (Nov. 13, 2013), http://www.publicknowledge.org/news-blog/blogs/impact-patent-troll-demand-letters ("Demand letters are letters patent owners send to unsuspecting businesses or individuals alleging patent infringement and threatening a lawsuit.").

[150] *See generally The Impact of Patent Assertion Entities on Innovation and the Economy: Hearing Before the H. Subcomm. on Oversight and Investigations of the H. Comm. on Energy and Commerce*, 113th Congress 3–5 (2013) [hereinafter PAE Hearing Testimony] (statement of Charles Duan, Director, Patent Reform Project, Public Knowledge), *available at* http://docs.house.gov/meetings/IF/IF02/20131114/101483/HHRG-113-IF02-Wstate-DuanC-20131114.pdf (discussing these various abusive demand letter practices).

[151] *See* William H. Sorrell, Vt. Attorney Gen. & Jon Bruning, Neb. Attorney Gen., *Vermont and Nebraska Attorneys General Take Patent Trolls Head On*, NAAGAZETTE (Nat'l Ass'n of Attorneys Gen., Wash., D.C.), Oct. 29, 2013, 3–5, *available at* http://www.naag.org/assets/files/pdf/gazette/7-9-10.Gazette.pdf.

[152] *See* PAE Hearing Testimony, *supra* note 150, at 6; Agency Information Collection Activities; Proposed Collection; Comment Request, 78 Fed. Reg. 61,352, 61,353 (Fed. Trade Comm'n Oct. 3, 2013) ("While workshop panelists and commenters identified potential harms and efficiencies of [patent assertion entity] activity, they noted a lack of empirical data in this area, and recommended that the Federal Trade Commission use its authority...to collect information on PAE acquisition, litigation, and licensing practices.").

[153] *See* PAE Hearing Testimony, *supra* note 150, at 9–10.

[154] *See id.* at 11–12.

Section 6.2

[155] *See* FED. R. CIV. P. 8(a)(2) (a complaint must include "a short and plain statement of the claim showing that the pleader is entitled to relief").

[156] *See* Bell Atl. Corp. v. Twombly, 550 U.S. 544, 559 (2007) (finding, because "the threat of discovery expense will push cost-conscious defendants to settle even anemic cases," that "it is only by taking care to require allegations that reach the level suggesting conspiracy that we can hope to avoid the potentially enormous expense of discovery in cases with no reasonably founded hope that the discovery process will reveal relevant evidence....").

[157] More specifically, Form 18 of the Appendix of Forms to the Federal Rules of Civil Procedure specifies a complaint that essentially only iden-

tifies the patents being infringed; the Federal Circuit has held that "to the extent that any conflict exists between *Twombly* (and its progeny) and the Forms regarding pleadings requirements, the Forms control." K-Tech Telecomms. v. Time Warner Cable, 714 F.3d 1277, 1283 (Fed. Cir. 2013); *see also* Dennis Crouch, *Federal Circuit Supports Bare-Bones Patent Complaints*, PATENTLY-O (Apr. 23, 2013), http://patentlyo.com/patent/2013/04/federal-circuit-supports-bare-bones-patent-complaints.html.

[158] Macronix Int'l Co. v. Spansion Inc., No. 3:13-cv-679, 2014 U.S. Dist. LEXIS 31465, at *17 (E.D. Va. Mar. 10, 2014), *available at* http://scholar.google.com/scholar_case?case=5992875037084942788 ("[Rejecting Form 18] will serve to winnow out weak (or even baseless) claims and will protect defendants from the need to prepare defenses for the many claims that inevitably fall by the way side in patent cases. That also will serve to reduce the expense and burden of this kind of litigation to both parties which, like the antitrust litigation in *Twombly*, is onerous.").

Section 6.3

[159] Jim Kerstetter, *How Much Is that Patent Lawsuit Going to Cost You?*, CNET NEWS (Apr. 5, 2014), http://news.cnet.com/8301-32973_3-57409792-296/how-much-is-that-patent-lawsuit-going-to-cost-you/ (attorney fees for a fully litigated case are between $650,000 and $5 million).

[160] Colleen Chien, *Patent Trolls by the Numbers*, PATENTLY-O (Mar. 14, 2013), http://patentlyo.com/patent/2013/03/chien-patent-trolls.html.

[161] *See* Section 4.3 *supra* p. 21.

[162] *See* Innovation Act, H.R. 3309, 113th Cong. sec. 6(a)(2) (as referred to Senate, Dec. 9, 2013); Patent Abuse Reduction Act, S. 1013, 113th Cong. sec. 4, § 300(a)(1) (2013); Patent Litigation and Innovation Act, H.R. 2639, 113th Cong. sec. 5, § 300A (2013).

[163] U.S. GOV'T ACCOUNTABILITY OFFICE, *supra* note 125, at 38; *see also id.* at 37–38 ("One judge that we spoke to said that only a few of the documents in discovery are actually used at trial—often less than one document in 10,000....").

Section 6.4

[164] Where the patent owner is an operating company, the patent owner may alternately receive "lost profits," intended to be a computation of

what the patent owner would have received absent infringement. But the reasonable royalty is always a floor, or lower bound, on the award to a patent owner. *See* 35 U.S.C. § 284 (2013). The reasonable royalty is by far the most common award. PRICEWATERHOUSECOOPERS, 2013 PATENT LITIGATION STUDY: BIG CASES MAKE HEADLINES, WHILE PATENT CASES PROLIFERATE 11 (2013), *available at* http://www.pwc.com/en_us/us/forensic-services/publications/assets/2013-patent-litigation-study.pdf.

[165] *See* John C. Jarosz & Michael J. Chapman, *The Hypothetical Negotiation and Reasonable Royalty Damages: The Tail Wagging the Dog*, 16 STAN. TECH. L. REV. 769, 782–83 (2013), http://stlr.stanford.edu/pdf/royaltydamages.pdf.

[166] *See, e.g.*, Mark A. Lemley & Carl Shapiro, *Patent Holdup and Royalty Stacking*, 85 TEX. L. REV. 1991, 1996, 1999 (2007), http://faculty.haas.berkeley.edu/shapiro/stacking.pdf (defining the "benchmark royalty rate" as proportional to the "*Value* per unit of the patented feature to the downstream firm in comparison with the next best alternative technology).

[167] *See* Chao, *supra* note 127, at 122–24.

[168] *See* Ga.-Pac. Corp. v. U.S. Plywood Corp., 318 F. Supp. 1116, 1120 (S.D.N.Y. 1970).

[169] *See, e.g.*, Christopher B. Seaman, *Reconsidering the* Georgia-Pacific *Standard for Reasonable Royalty Patent Damages*, 2010 BYU L. REV. 1661, 1703, http://www.law2.byu.edu/lawreview/archives/2010/5/05Seaman.pdf ("Such broad, multifactor tests have been criticized as being poorly designed and containing duplicative or overlapping factors, which can lead to unpredictable results.").

[170] *See* Uniloc USA, Inc. v. Microsoft Corp., 632 F. 3d 1292, 1314–15 (Fed. Cir. 2011) ("[T]his court has passively tolerated [the 25 percent rule's] use....").

[171] *See* Love & Yoon, *supra* note 126, at 1635.

[172] *Uniloc USA, Inc.*, 632 F. 3d at 1315 ("This court now holds as a matter of Federal Circuit law that the 25 percent rule of thumb is a fundamentally flawed tool for determining a baseline royalty rate in a hypothetical negotiation.").

Section 6.5

[173] *Ex parte* reexamination enables a third party to ask the Patent Office to reconsider a patent, but does not permit the third party to participate in the proceeding. *See* 35 U.S.C. §§ 302–307 (2013); MPEP, *supra* note 20, § 2209. Post grant review, *inter partes* review, and covered business methods review all permit the third party to participate in the proceeding; the three procedures differ in when they may be filed, what patents they may be filed on, and the particular questions for reconsideration that may be presented to the Patent Office. *See* 35 U.S.C. §§ 311–319 (inter partes review); §§ 321–329 (post grant review); America Invents Act, Pub. L. No. 112-29, sec. 18, 125 Stat. 284, 329–31 (2011) (covered business methods program); Changes to Implement Inter Partes Review Proceedings, Post-Grant Review Proceedings, and Transitional Program for Covered Business Method Patents, 77 Fed. Reg. 48,680 (2012) (to be codified at 37 C.F.R. pt. 42).

[174] Thomas G. Southard & Paul F. Prestia, *Economics and Logic of Patent Litigation Versus Post Grant/Inter Partes Patent Review*, RATNERPRESTIA (Oct. 3, 2012), *available at* http://ratnerprestia.com/220?article=485 ("In light of these figures, challenging patent validity in a district court proceeding is likely to be a far more expensive proposition than contesting validity in the PTO modified proceedings.").

[175] Kimberly A. Moore, *Judges, Juries, and Patent Cases—An Empirical Peek Inside the Black Box*, 99 MICH. L. REV. 365, 409 (2000) ("Closer scrutiny of judge and jury decisionmaking elucidates differences which could implicate flaws in juror comprehension."); Kimberly A. Moore, *Are District Court Judges Equipped to Resolve Patent Cases?*, 15 HARV. J.L. & TECH. 1, 7 (2001) ("[F]ew district court judges are one of ordinary skill in the technology of the invention.").

[176] *See, e.g.*, 35 U.S.C. § 321(a) ("[A] person who is not the owner of a patent may file with the Office a petition to institute a post-grant review of the patent.").

[177] The mechanism for a party to bring a district court lawsuit against a patent owner is called a "declaratory judgment action," and such an action can only be brought where "the facts alleged, under all the circumstances, show that there is a substantial controversy, between parties having adverse legal interests, of sufficient immediacy and reality to warrant the issuance of a declaratory judgment." Medimmune, Inc. v. Genentech, Inc.,

549 U.S. 118, 127 (2007) (quoting Md. Cas. Co. v. Pac. Coal & Oil Co., 312 U.S. 270, 273 (1941)).

[178] *See, e.g.,* Robert P. Greenspoon, *Is the United States Finally Ready for a Patent Small Claims Court?*, 10 MINN. J.L. SCI. & TECH. 549 (2009), *available at* http://mjlst.umn.edu/prod/groups/ahc/@pub/@ahc/@mjlst/documents/asset/ahc_asset_366031.pdf.

[179] *E.g.,* Patents Act 1990, ch. 12, sec. 133 (Austl.), *available at* http://www.austlii.edu.au/au/legis/cth/consol_act/pa1990109/.

[180] *E.g.,* 17 U.S.C. § 115 (2013) (compulsory licenses for phonorecords of nondramatic musical works).

Section 6.6

[181] This section is generally adapted from Charles Duan, *Patent Trolls Are The Economy-Suffocating Exception To The 'No Free Lunch' Rule*, FORBES, Nov. 15, 2013, http://www.forbes.com/sites/realspin/2013/11/15/patent-trolls-are-the-economy-suffocating-exception-to-the-no-free-lunch-rule/.

[182] *See* PRICEWATERHOUSECOOPERS, *supra* note 164, at 7 chart 2b.

[183] Jim Kerstetter, *How Much Is that Patent Lawsuit Going to Cost You?*, CNET NEWS (Apr. 5, 2014), http://news.cnet.com/8301-32973_3-57409792-296/how-much-is-that-patent-lawsuit-going-to-cost-you/.

[184] Saving High-Tech Innovators from Egregious Legal Disputes Act, H.R. 845, 113th Cong. sec. 2, § 285A(a)(4) (2013); Patent Abuse Reduction Act, S. 1013, 113th Cong. sec. 5, § 285(a) (2013); Innovation Act, H.R. 3309, 113th Cong. sec. 3(b)(1), § 285(a) (as referred to Senate, Dec. 9, 2013); Patent Litigation Integrity Act, S. 1612, 113th Cong. (2013).

Section 7

[185] *E.g.,* Precision Instrument Mfg. Co. v. Auto. Maint. Mach. Co., 324 U.S. 806, 816 (1945) ("[A] patent is an exception to the general rule against monopolies and to the right to access to a free and open market."), *quoted in* Walker Process Equip., Inc. v. Food Mach. & Chem. Corp., 382 U.S. 172, 177 (1965).

[186] Fed. Trade Comm'n v. Actavis, Inc., 133 S. Ct. 2223, 2231 (2013).

[187] *See, e.g., id.* at 2238–39 (Roberts, J., dissenting).

[188] *See id.* at 2231; *see also* Herbert Hovenkamp, *Consumer Welfare In Competition And Intellectual Property Law*, 9 COMPETITION POL'Y INT'L 53, 60 (2013) ("Consumer harm does result when the intellectual property system provides more exclusionary power than is necessary to develop some new thing, or when it excludes without providing anything new at all.").

Section 7.1

[189] *See, e.g.,* U.S. DEP'T OF JUSTICE & FED. TRADE COMM'N, ANTITRUST ENFORCEMENT AND INTELLECTUAL PROPERTY RIGHTS: PROMOTING INNOVATION AND COMPETITION 33 (2007), *available at* http://www.usdoj.gov/atr/public/hearings/ip/222655.pdf ("Standards make networks, such as the Internet and wireless telecommunications, more valuable by allowing products to interoperate.").

[190] *See id.* at 46–47.

[191] *See* Mark A. Lemley & Carl Shapiro, *A Simple Approach to Setting Reasonable Royalties for Standard-Essential Patents*, 28 BERKELEY TECH. L.J. 1135, 1137 (2013) ("FRAND commitments serve two primary goals: (1) to promote the standard by assuring companies that they will not be blocked from bringing their products to market..., and (2) to provide reasonable rewards to those who have invested in research and development to develop the technology used by the standard."); Anne Layne-Farrar et al., *Pricing Patents for Licensing in Standard-Setting Organizations: Making Sense of FRAND Commitments*, 74 ANTITRUST L.J. 671, 672 (2007) ("FRAND commitments are meant to address a prominent concern in standard setting: the adoption of a technology into a major standard could confer substantial market power, or substantially increased market power, on its owner.").

[192] *See, e.g.,* Layne-Farrar et al., *supra* note 191, at 672; Lemley & Shapiro, *supra* note 191, at 1160 ("Parties have spent a great deal of time litigating the question of whether one or both sides have breached a FRAND commitment."). The term "RAND" is essentially interchangeable with FRAND.

[193] *See* U.S. Dep't of Justice & U.S. Patent & Trademark Office, *Policy Statement on Remedies for Standards-Essential Patents Subject to Voluntary F/RAND Commitments* 6 (Jan. 8, 2013), http://www.justice.gov/atr/public/guidelines/290994.pdf ("A patent owner's voluntary F/RAND commitments may also affect the appropriate choice of remedy for infringe-

ment of a valid and enforceable standards-essential patent. In some circumstances, the remedy of an injunction or exclusion order may be inconsistent with the public interest.").

[194] *See* David Balto, *Using the Antitrust Laws to Police Patent Privateering*, PATENTLY-O (June 3, 2013), http://patentlyo.com/patent/2013/06/guest-post-on-using-the-antitrust-laws-to-police-patent-privateering.html ("Privateering lets operating companies evade...'FRAND or other licensing commitments,' and provides a method for 'strategic outsourcing to PAEs to hinder rivals.'").

Section 7.2

[195] *See* RPX Corp., Registration Statement (Form S-1), at 59 (Sept. 2, 2011).

[196] Several Supreme Court justices recognized the risk of injunctions being used to demand an excessively high licensing fee. *See* eBay Inc. v. MercExchange, LLC, 547 U.S. 388, 396–97 (2006) (recognizing that, for non-practicing entities, "an injunction, and the potentially serious sanctions arising from its violation, can be employed as a bargaining tool to charge exorbitant fees to companies that seek to buy licenses to practice the patent.").

[197] U.S. DEP'T OF JUSTICE & FED. TRADE COMM'N, *supra* note 189, at 38 ("A holder of IP incorporated into a standard can exploit its position if it is costly for users of the standard to switch to a different technology after the standard is set."); Lemley & Shapiro, *supra* note 166, at 1992–93 ("The threat that a patent holder will obtain an injunction that will force the downstream producer to pull its product from the market can be very powerful....Injunction threats often involve a strong element of *holdup* in the common circumstance in which the defendant has already invested heavily to design, manufacture, market, and sell the product with the allegedly infringing feature.").

[198] *See* Lemley & Shapiro, *supra* note 166, at 1993 ("Royalty stacking refers to situations in which a single product potentially infringes on many patents, and thus may bear multiple royalty burdens.").

[199] *See id.* at 2013 ("the recent surge in patenting, especially in the information technology industry where royalty stacking is a serious concern,

these overcharges, when aggregated, can lead to a very significant cost burden on producers."); section 6.4 *supra* p. 33.

B Bibliography

Introduction

James Bessen & Michael J. Meurer, *The Direct Costs from NPE Disputes*, 99 CORNELL L. REV. (forthcoming 2014), http://www.bu.edu/law/faculty/scholarship/workingpapers/revcov.html 45

MICHELE BOLDRIN & DAVID K. LEVINE, AGAINST INTELLECTUAL MONOPOLY (2008), *available at* http://www.dklevine.com/general/intellectual/againstfinal.htm 46

Bonito Boats, Inc. v. Thunder Craft Boats, Inc., 489 U.S. 141 (1989) . . 45

COLLEEN V. CHIEN, NEW AM. FOUND., PATENT ASSERTION AND STARTUP INNOVATION (2013), http://www.newamerica.net/publications/policy/patent_assertion_and_startup_innovation 45, 52

Diamond v. Chakrabarty, 447 U.S. 303 (1980) 45

Mark A. Lemley, *The Myth of the Sole Inventor*, 110 MICH. L. REV. 709 (2012) 46, 49, 54, 56

Matt Levy, *Patent Progress's Guide to Patent Reform Legislation* (Nov. 19, 2013), http://www.patentprogress.org/2013/11/19/patent-progresss-guide-to-patent-reform-legislation/ 45

Adam Mossoff, *Policy Debates on Patents Should Focus on Facts, Not Rhetoric*, FORBES, Dec. 18, 2012, http://www.forbes.com/sites/realspin/2012/12/18/policy-debates-on-patents-should-focus-on-facts-not-rhetoric/ 46

Michael Schrage, *Archaic Patent Laws Need to Be Rewritten*, L.A. TIMES, Oct. 24, 1991, at D1, *available at* http://articles.latimes.com/1991-10-24/business/fi-436_1_intellectual-property-protection . . . 45

Joff Wild, *The Real Inventors of the Term "Patent Troll" Revealed*, INTELLECTUAL ASSET MANAGEMENT, Aug. 22, 2008, http://www.iam-magazine.com/blog/detail.aspx?g=cff2afd3-c24e-42e5-aa68-a4b4e7524177 45

Background

Colleen V. Chien, *From Arms Race to Marketplace: The Complex Patent Ecosystem and Its Implications for the Patent System*, 62 HASTINGS L.J. 297 (2010), *available at* http://www.hastingslawjournal.org/wp-content/uploads/2011/02/Chien_62-HLJ-297.pdf 48

Vincenzo Denicolò & Luigi Alberto Franzoni, *The Contract Theory of Patents*, 23 INT'L REV. L. & ECON. 365 (2003), *available at* http://www2.dse.unibo.it/franzoni/contract.pdf 46

John F. Duffy, *Reviving the Paper Patent Doctrine*, 98 CORNELL L. REV. 1359 (2013), *available at* http://cornelllawreview.org/files/2013/10/98CLR1359.pdf 49

Eldred v. Ashcroft, 537 U.S. 186 (2003) 47

FED. TRADE COMM'N, TO PROMOTE INNOVATION: THE PROPER BALANCE OF COMPETITION AND PATENT LAW AND POLICY (2003), *available at* http://www.ftc.gov/sites/default/files/documents/reports/promote-innovation-proper-balance-competition-and-patent-law-and-policy/innovationrpt.pdf 48, 53

Jeanne C. Fromer, *Patent Disclosure*, 94 IOWA L. REV. 539 (2009) . . 46, 49

Christopher A. Harkins, *Fending Off Paper Patents and Patent Trolls: A Novel "Cold Fusion" Defense Because Changing Times Demand It*, 17 ALB. L.J. SCI. & TECH. 407 (2007), *available at* http://www.brinksgilson.com/files/219.pdf 48

Sara Jeruss et al., *The America Invents Act 500: Effects of Patent Monetization Entities on US Litigation*, 11 DUKE L. & TECH. REV. 357 (2012), *available at* http://scholarship.law.duke.edu/dltr/vol11/iss2/6/ 48

Mark A. Lemley & Douglas Melamed, *Missing the Forest for the Trolls*, 113 COLUM. L. REV. 2117 (2013), *available at* http://columbialawreview.org/missing-the-forest-for-the-trolls-3/ 49

Letter from Thomas Jefferson, to Isaac McPherson (Aug. 13, 1813), *available at* http://press-pubs.uchicago.edu/founders/documents/a1_8_8s12.html, *reprinted in* 3 THE FOUNDERS' CONSTITUTION art. 1, § 8, cl. 8, document 12 (Philip B. Kurland & Ralph Lerner eds., 1987) . . 47

Markman v. Westview Instruments, Inc., 517 U.S. 370 (1996) . . . 48, 58

Markman v. Westview Instruments, Inc., 52 F.3d 967 (Fed. Cir. 1995) 48

Adam Mossoff, *The Myth of the "Patent Troll" Litigation Explosion*, CENTER FOR THE PROTECTION OF INTELLECTUAL PROPERTY (Aug. 12, 2013), http://cpip.gmu.edu/2013/08/12/the-myth-of-the-patent-troll-litigation-explosion/ 48

Kirsten Osenga, *Linguistics and Patent Claim Construction*, 38 RUTGERS L.J. 61 (2006) 47–48

PATENT LOCAL RULES § 4 (U.S. Dist. Court for the N. Dist. of Cal. 2009), *available at* http://www.cand.uscourts.gov/localrules/patent 48

Pennock v. Dialogue, 27 U.S. (2 Pet.) 1 (1829) 47

THE FOUNDERS' CONSTITUTION (Philip B. Kurland & Ralph Lerner eds., 1987) 47

U.S. CONST. art. 1, § 8, cl. 8 . . . . 47, 56

U.S. PATENT & TRADEMARK OFFICE, MANUAL OF PATENT EXAMINING PROCEDURE (8th ed., 9th rev. 2012) 47–48, 54, 57–58, 67

Accounting for All Inventors

Sara-Jayne Adams, *Quality Is the Key to a Bright Patent Future*, INTELL. ASSET MGMT., Apr./May 2008, at 55, *available at* http://www.iam-magazine.com/Issues/Article.ashx?g=7ec06ce7-8c64-4402-9222-f79e3aaaf171 54

Alice Corp. v. CLS Bank Int'l, 134 S. Ct. 734 (2013) 53

YOCHAI BENKLER, THE WEALTH OF NETWORKS: HOW SOCIAL PRODUCTION TRANSFORMS MARKETS AND FREEDOM (2006), *available at* http://www.benkler.org/Benkler_Wealth_Of_Networks.pdf 51

Bilski v. Kappos, 130 S. Ct. 3218 (2010) 54

Brief of *Amici Curiae* Checkpoint Software, Inc., et al., in Support of Respondents, Alice Corp. Pty. Ltd. v. CLS Bank Int'l, No. 13-298 (U.S. Feb. 27, 2014) 49

Jon Brodkin, *How Red Hat Killed Its Core Product—And Became a Billion-Dollar Business*, ARS TECHNICA, Feb. 28, 2012, http://arstechnica.com/business/2012/02/how-red-hat-killed-its-core-productand-became-a-billion-dollar-business/ 51

Zechariah Chafee, Jr., *Reflections on the Law of Copyright: I*, 45 COLUM. L. REV. 503 (1945) 54

COLLEEN V. CHIEN, NEW AM. FOUND., PATENT ASSERTION AND STARTUP INNOVATION (2013), http://www.newamerica.net/publications/policy/patent_assertion_and_startup_innovation 45, 52

CLS Bank Int'l v. Alice Corp., 717 F.3d 1269 (Fed. Cir. 2013) 53

Charles Duan, Pub. Knowledge, *Comments of Public Knowledge, the Electronic Frontier Foundation, and Engine Advocacy on Prior Art Resources for Use in the Examination of Software-Related Patent Applications* (Mar. 17, 2014), *available at* https://www.eff.org/files/2014/03/17/comments_to_pto_from_public_knowledge_eff_engine.pdf 55

Rebecca S. Eisenberg, *Patents and the Progress of Science: Exclusive Rights and Experimental Use*, 56 U. CHI. L. REV. 1017 (1989) 53

Rebecca S. Eisenberg, *The Role of the FDA in Innovation Policy*, 13 MICH. TELECOMM. & TECH. L. REV. 345 (2007), *available at* http://www.mttlr.org/volthirteen/eisenberg.pdf 49

FED. TRADE COMM'N, TO PROMOTE INNOVATION: THE PROPER BALANCE OF COMPETITION AND PATENT LAW AND POLICY (2003), *available at* http://www.ftc.gov/sites/default/files/documents/reports/promote-innovation-proper-balance-competition-and-patent-law-and-policy/innovationrpt.pdf 48, 53

Jeanne C. Fromer, *Patent Disclosure*, 94 IOWA L. REV. 539 (2009) . . 46, 49

Funk Bros. Seed Co. v. Kalo Inoculant Co., 333 U.S. 127 (1948) 54

Great Atl. & Pac. Tea Co. v. Supermarket Equip. Corp., 340 U.S. 147 (1950) 54

Daniel J. Hemel & Lisa Larrimore Ouellette, *Beyond the Patents—Prizes Debate*, 92 TEX. L. REV. 304 (2013), *available at* http://www.texaslrev.com/wp-content/uploads/HemelOuellette.pdf 52

In re Rosuvastatin Calcium Patent Litig., 703 F.3d 511 (Fed. Cir. 2012) 53

Kewanee Oil Co. v. Bicron Corp., 416 U.S. 470 (1974) 50

Kinetic Concepts, Inc. v. Smith & Nephew, Inc., 688 F.3d 1342 (Fed. Cir. 2012) 55

Michael Kremer, *Patent Buyouts: A Mechanism for Encouraging Innovation*, 113 THE QUARTERLY JOURNAL OF ECONOMICS 1137 (1998) .. 51

KSR Int'l Co. v. Teleflex Inc., 550 U.S. 398 (2007) 15, 55

Mark A. Lemley, *Reconceiving Patents in the Age of Venture Capital*, 4 J. SMALL & EMERGING BUS. L. 137 (2000) 50

Mark A. Lemley, *The Myth of the Sole Inventor*, 110 MICH. L. REV. 709 (2012) 46, 49, 54, 56

Letter from Isaac Newton, to Robert Hooke (Feb. 5, 1675), *available at* http://digitallibrary.hsp.org/index.php/Detail/Object/Show/object_id/9565 54

Steven Levy, *Y Combinator Is Boot Camp for Startups*, WIRED (May 17, 2011), http://www.wired.com/magazine/2011/05/ff_ycombinator/ 50

MICHAEL MANDEL, WHERE THE JOBS ARE: THE APP ECONOMY (2012) ... 50

Peter S. Menell, *Indirect Copyright Liability and Technological Innovation*, 32 COLUM. J.L. & ARTS 375 (2009) 50

Adam Messinger, *Introducing the Innovator's Patent Agreement*, THE OFFICIAL TWITTER BLOG (Apr. 17, 2012), https://blog.twitter.com/2012/introducing-innovators-patent-agreement 53

Alfred Bernhard Nobel, *Alfred Nobel's Will* (Nov. 27, 1895), http://www.nobelprize.org/alfred_nobel/will/will-full.html 52

Beth Simone Noveck, *"Peer to Patent": Collective Intelligence, Open Review, and Patent Reform*, 20 HARV. J.L. & TECH. 123 (2006) 54

ANDREAS PAPPAS, VISIONMOBILE LTD., APP ECONOMY FORECASTS 2013–2016 (2013) 50

Press Release, Dep't of Justice, *CPTN Holdings LLC and Novell Inc. Change Deal in Order to Address Department of Justice's Open Source Concerns* (Apr. 20, 2011), *available at* http://www.justice.gov/opa/pr/2011/April/11-at-491.html 52

Press Release, Karen Duffin, Bite Commc'ns for OSRM, *Results of First-Ever Linux Patent Review Announced, Patent Insurance Offered by Open Source Risk Management* (Aug. 2, 2004), http://www.osriskmanagement.com/press_releases/press_release_080204.pdf 52

Press Release, Elec. Frontier Found., *EFF Files Challenge with Patent Office Against Troll's Podcasting Patent* (Oct. 16, 2013), https://www.eff.org/press/releases/eff-files-challenge-patent-office-against-trolls-podcasting-patent 53

Press Release, Office of the Press Sec'y, The White House, *Fact Sheet—Executive Actions: Answering the President's Call to Strengthen Our Patent System and Foster Innovation* (Feb. 20, 2014), http://www.whitehouse.gov/the-press-office/2014/02/20/fact-sheet-executive-actions-answering-president-s-call-strengthen-our-p 54, 58

Press Release, Peter Pappas, U.S. Patent & Trademark Office, *USPTO Launches Second Peer To Patent Pilot in Collaboration with New York Law School* (Oct. 19, 2010), http://www.uspto.gov/news/pr/2010/10_50.jsp 54

Gene Quinn, *The Cost of Obtaining a Patent in the US*, IPWATCHDOG (Jan. 28, 2011), http://www.ipwatchdog.com/2011/01/28/the-cost-of-obtaining-patent/ 50

ERIC S. RAYMOND, THE CATHEDRAL AND THE BAZAAR: MUSINGS ON LINUX AND OPEN SOURCE BY AN ACCIDENTAL REVOLUTIONARY (rev. ed. 2001) 51

Request for Comments and Notice of Roundtable Event on the Use of Crowdsourcing and Third-Party Preissuance Submissions to Identify Relevant Prior Art, 79 Fed. Reg. 15,319 (U.S. Patent & Trademark Office 2014) 55

ERIC RIES, THE LEAN STARTUP: HOW TODAY'S ENTREPRENEURS USE CONTINUOUS INNOVATION TO CREATE RADICALLY SUCCESSFUL BUSINESSES (2011) 51

Jason Schultz & Jennifer M. Urban, *Protecting Open Innovation: The Defensive Patent License as a New Approach to Patent Threats, Transaction Costs, and Tactical Disarmament*, 26 HARV. J.L. & TECH. 1 (2012), *available at* http://jolt.law.harvard.edu/articles/pdf/v26/26HarvJLTech1.pdf 51, 53

Wendy Seltzer, *Software Patents and/or Software Development*, 78 BROOKLYN L. REV. 929 (2013), *available at* http://www.brooklaw.edu/~/media/PDF/LawJournals/BLR_PDF/blr_v78iii.ashx 49–50

Sony Corp. of Am. v. Universal City Studios, Inc., 464 U.S. 417 (1984) . . 54

RICHARD M. STALLMAN, FREE SOFTWARE, FREE SOCIETY (2d ed. 2010), *available at* http://www.gnu.org/doc/fsfs-ii-2.pdf 51

Richard Stallman, *Why Upgrade to GPLv3* (July 29, 2013), https://www.gnu.org/licenses/rms-why-gplv3.html 53

Joseph Stiglitz, *Give Prizes Not Patents*, NEW SCIENTIST, Sept. 16, 2006, at 21, *available at* http://www2.gsb.columbia.edu/faculty/jstiglitz/download/2006_New_Scientist.pdf 51

The GNU General Public License v.3.0 (June 29, 2007), http://www.gnu.org/licenses/gpl.html 53

U.S. PATENT & TRADEMARK OFFICE, MANUAL OF PATENT EXAMINING PROCEDURE (8th ed., 9th rev. 2012) 47–48, 54, 57–58, 67

Daniel J. Weitzner, *W3C Patent Policy*, W3.ORG (Feb. 5, 2004), http://www.w3.org/Consortium/Patent-Policy-20040205/ 52

When Patents Attack!, THIS AMERICAN LIFE (July 22, 2011), http://www.thisamericanlife.org / radio - archives / episode / 441 / when - patents-attack 52

Whittemore v. Cutter, 29 F. Cas. 1120 (C.C.D. Mass. 1813) 53

ROBERT H. ZAKON, REQUEST FOR COMMENTS 2235: HOBBES' INTERNET TIMELINE (1997), http://tools.ietf.org/html/rfc2235 52

Clarity of Patents

37 C.F.R. § 1.133 (2013) 57

37 C.F.R. § 1.2 (2013) 57

James Bessen et al., *The Private and Social Costs of Patent Trolls*, REGULATION, Winter 2011–2012, at 26, http://object.cato.org/sites/cato.org/files/serials/files/regulation/2012/5/v34n4-1.pdf 56

JAMES BESSEN & MICHAEL J. MEURER, PATENT FAILURE: HOW JUDGES, BUREAUCRATS, AND LAWYERS PUT INNOVATORS AT RISK (2008) 57

Brief of *Amicus Curiae* Public Knowledge in Support of Petitioner, WildTangent, Inc. v. Ultramercial, LLC, No. 13-255 (June 21, 2013) . . 58

Brief of Public Knowledge and the Electronic Frontier Foundation as *Amici Curiae* in Support of Petitioner, Nautilus, Inc. v. Biosig Instruments, Inc., No. 13-369 (U.S. Oct. 23, 2013) 55

Cybor Corp. v. FAS Techs., Inc., 138 F.3d 1448 (Fed. Cir. 1998) 58

Datamize, LLC v. Plumtree Software, Inc., 417 F.3d 1342 (Fed. Cir. 2005) 56

Charles Duan, *Comments of Public Knowledge and the Electronic Frontier Foundation on the United States Patent and Trademark Office Software Partnership Meeting* (Oct. 24, 2013), http://www.uspto.gov/patents/init_events/swglossary_a_eff_2013oct24.pdf . . . 58

Elec. Frontier Found., *Comments of EFF on Enhancement of Quality of Software-Related Patents* (Apr. 15, 2013), *available at* https://www.eff.org/files/eff_comments_on_enhancement_of_quality_of_software-related_patents.pdf 57

Exxon Research & Eng'g Co. v. United States, 265 F.3d 1371 (Fed. Cir. 2001) 56

FED. TRADE COMM'N, THE EVOLVING IP MARKETPLACE: ALIGNING PATENT NOTICE AND REMEDIES WITH COMPETITION (2011) 56, 63

Gen. Elec. Corp. v. Wabash Appliance Corp., 304 U.S. 364 (1938) . . . 56

PHIL GOLDBERG, PROGRESSIVE POLICY INST., STUMPING PATENT TROLLS ON THE BRIDGE TO INNOVATION (2013) 56, 63

Kirk M. Hartung, *Claim Construction: Another Matter of Chance and Confusion*, 88 J. PAT. & TRADEMARK OFF. SOC'Y 831 (2006) 56

Christa J. Laser, *A Definite Claim On Claim Indefiniteness*, 10 CHI.-KENT J. INTELL. PROP. 25 (2010) 56

Lemelson v. Gen. Mills, Inc., 968 F.2d 1202 (Fed. Cir. 1992) 57

Mark A. Lemley, *The Myth of the Sole Inventor*, 110 MICH. L. REV. 709 (2012) 46, 49, 54, 56

Mark A. Lemley & Kimberly A. Moore, *Ending Abuse of Patent Continuations*, 84 B.U. L. REV. 63 (2004) 59

Susan Lynch, *Interviewing Patent Examiners—Advantageous or Disastrous?* (Feb. 15, 2006), http://www.ipfrontline.com/depts/article.aspx?id=721&deptid=4 57

Markman v. Westview Instruments, Inc., 517 U.S. 370 (1996) . . . 48, 58

McClain v. Ortmayer, 141 U.S. 419 (1891) 56

Christina Mulligan & Timothy B. Lee, *Scaling the Patent System*, 68 N.Y.U. ANN. SURV. AM. L. 289 (2012) 56

N. DIST. OF CAL. PATENT LOCAL RULES §§ 4-1 to -7 (2009), *available at* http://www.cand.uscourts.gov/localrules/patent 58

Matthew R. Osenga, *Interviews with Patent Examiners* (Apr. 30, 2012), http://inventivestep.net/2012/04/30/interviews-with-patent-examiners/. 57

Lisa Larrimore Ouellette, *Do Patents Disclose Useful Information?*, 25 HARV. J.L. & TECH. 545 (2012) 55

Phillips v. AWH Corp., 415 F.3d 1303 (Fed. Cir. 2005) 57–58

Press Release, Office of the Press Sec'y, The White House, *Fact Sheet—Executive Actions: Answering the President's Call to Strengthen Our Patent System and Foster Innovation* (Feb. 20, 2014), http://www.whitehouse.gov/the-press-office/2014/02/20/fact-sheet-executive-actions-answering-president-s-call-strengthen-our-p 54, 58

David Segal, *Has Patent, Will Sue: An Alert to Corporate America*, N.Y. TIMES, July 14, 2013, at BU1 56

Carl Shapiro, *Navigating the Patent Thicket: Cross Licenses, Patent Pools, and Standard Setting*, *in* 1 INNOVATION POLICY AND THE ECONOMY 119 (Adam B. Jaffe et al. eds., 2001) 59

Svetlana Sheremetyeva, *Natural Language Analysis of Patent Claims*, 20 PROC. ACL-2003 WORKSHOP ON PAT. CORPUS PROCESSING 66 (2003), *available at* http://acl.ldc.upenn.edu/W/W03/W03-2008.pdf 59

Rich Steeves, *New Report Examines the Economic Cost of Patent Trolls*, INSIDECOUNSEL (Oct. 11, 2013), http://www.insidecounsel.com/2013/10/11/new-report-examines-the-economic-cost-of-patent-tr 55

Tafas v. Doll, 559 F.3d 1345 (Fed. Cir. 2009) 59

Tafas v. Kappos, 586 F.3d 1369 (Fed. Cir. 2009) 59

U.S. CONST. art. 1, § 8, cl. 8 . . . . 47, 56

U.S. Patent No. 7,480,627 (filed Oct. 10, 2000) 56

U.S. PATENT & TRADEMARK OFFICE, MANUAL OF PATENT EXAMINING PROCEDURE (8th ed., 9th rev. 2012) 47–48, 54, 57–58, 67

United Carbon Co. v. Binney & Smith Co., 317 U.S. 228 (1942) 56

Rob Weir, *How Not to Read a Patent* (Aug. 13, 2009), http://www.robweir.com/blog/2009/08/how-not-to-read-patent.html 55

Targeting the Right Parties

James Bessen, *The Patent Troll Crisis Is Really a Software Patent Crisis*, WASHINGTON POST: THE SWITCH (Sept. 3, 2013), http://www.washingtonpost.com/blogs/the-switch/wp/2013/09/03/the-patent-troll-crisis-is-really-a-software-patent-crisis/ 62

ERIK BRYNJOLFSSON & ADAM SAUNDERS, WIRED FOR INNOVATION: HOW INFORMATION TECHNOLOGY IS RESHAPING THE ECONOMY (2010) 62

David A. Burton, *Software Developers Want Changes in Patent and Copyright Law*, 3 MICH. TELECOMM. & TECH. L. REV. 87 (1996), http://www.mttlr.org/voltwo/burton.pdf 62

Bernard Chao, *The Case for Contribution in Patent Law*, 80 U. CIN. L. REV. 113 (2011), http://scholarship.law.uc.edu/cgi/viewcontent.cgi?article=1083&context=uclr 60–61, 66

Colleen V. Chien, *Reforming Software Patents*, 50 HOUS. L. REV. 325 (2012), *available at* http://www.houstonlawreview.org/wp-content/uploads/2013/02/2-Chien.pdf 60, 62

Codex Corp. v. Milgo Elec. Corp., 553 F.2d 735 (1st Cir. 1977) 61

Dennis Crouch, *Capturing the Consumer Surplus Through Downstream Licensing and Infringement Lawsuits*, PATENTLY-O (Dec. 6, 2013), http://patentlyo.com/patent/2013/12/capturing-the-consumer-surplus-through-downstream-licensing-and-infringement-lawsuits.html 61

Earl W. Hayter, *The Patent System and Agrarian Discontent, 1875-1888*, 34 MISS. VALLEY HIST. REV. 59 (1947) 60

Innovation Act, H.R. 3309, 113th Cong. (as referred to Senate, Dec. 9, 2013) 61, 65, 68

Katz v. Lear Siegler, Inc., 909 F.2d 1459 (Fed. Cir. 1990) 61

Timothy B. Lee, *The Supreme Court Could Abolish Software Patents Next Year. Here's Why It Should*, WASHINGTON POST: THE SWITCH (Dec. 6, 2013), http://www.washingtonpost.com/blogs/the-switch/wp/2013/12/06/the-supreme-court-could-abolish-software-patents-next-year-heres-why-it-should/ 62

David Long & Matt Rizzolo, *Protecting "End Users" from Patent Infringement Actions*, INSIDECOUNSEL (Sept. 18, 2013), http://www.insidecounsel.com/2013/09/18/protecting-end-users-from-patent-infringement-acti 60

Brian J. Love & James C. Yoon, *Expanding Patent Law's Customer Suit Exception*, 93 B.U. L. REV. 1605 (2013), *available at* http://www.bu.edu/bulawreview/files/2013/10/LOVE-YOON_Expanding-Patent.pdf 60–62, 66

Joe Mullin, *Patent Trolls Want $1,000—for Using Scanners*, ARS TECHNICA (Jan. 2, 2013), http://arstechnica.com/tech-policy/2013/01/patent-trolls-want-1000-for-using-scanners/ 59

Patent Litigation and Innovation Act, H.R. 2639, 113th Cong. (2013) 62, 65

Patent Transparency and Improvements Act, S. 1720, 113th Cong. (2013) 61

John Ribeiro, *Cisco Reaches Agreement with Innovatio over Wi-Fi Patents*, PCWORLD (Feb. 7, 2014), http://www.pcworld.com/article/2095700/cisco-reaches-agreement-with-innovatio-over-wifi-patents.html 59

Alan Schoenbaum, *Immunize End Users from Patent Trolls*, RACKSPACE BLOG (Mar. 19, 2013), http://www.rackspace.com/blog/immunize-end-users-from-patent-trolls/ 61

Erik Slivka, *Lodsys Threatens to Sue App Store Developers Over In-App Purchases and Upgrade Links*, MACRUMORS (May 13, 2011), http://www.macrumors.com/2011/05/13/lodsys-threatens-to-sue-app-store-developers-over-purchase-links/ 59

U.S. GOV'T ACCOUNTABILITY OFFICE, GAO-13-465, INTELLECTUAL PROPERTY: ASSESSING FACTORS THAT AFFECT PATENT INFRINGEMENT LITIGATION COULD HELP IMPROVE PATENT QUALITY (2013), *available at* http://www.gao.gov/assets/660/657103.pdf 60, 62–63, 65

Heesun Wee, *The "Gold Rush" for 3-D Printing Patents* (Aug. 15, 2013), http://www.cnbc.com/id/100942655, CNBC.com 62

Avoiding Gamesmanship in Litigation

Agency Information Collection Activities; Proposed Collection; Comment Request, 78 Fed. Reg. 61,352 (Fed. Trade Comm'n Oct. 3, 2013) 64

John R. Allison et al., *Patent Quality and Settlement Among Repeat Patent Litigants*, 99 GEO. L.J. 677 (2011), *available at* http://georgetownlawjournal.org/files/pdf/99-3/AllisonLemleyWalker%2520677-712.PDF 63

America Invents Act, Pub. L. No. 112-29, 125 Stat. 284 (2011) 67

Bell Atl. Corp. v. Twombly, 550 U.S. 544 (2007) 64

Changes to Implement Inter Partes Review Proceedings, Post-Grant Review Proceedings, and Transitional Program for Covered Business Method Patents, 77 Fed. Reg. 48,680 (2012) (to be codified at 37 C.F.R. pt. 42) 67

Bernard Chao, *The Case for Contribution in Patent Law*, 80 U. CIN. L. REV. 113 (2011), http://scholarship.law.uc.edu/cgi/viewcontent.cgi?article=1083&context=uclr 60–61, 66

Colleen Chien, *Patent Trolls by the Numbers*, PATENTLY-O (Mar. 14, 2013), http://patentlyo.com/patent/2013/03/chien-patent-trolls.html 65

Dennis Crouch, *Federal Circuit Supports Bare-Bones Patent Complaints*, PATENTLY-O (Apr. 23, 2013), http://patentlyo.com/patent/2013/04/federal-circuit-supports-bare-bones-patent-complaints.html 65

Charles Duan, *Patent Trolls Are The Economy-Suffocating Exception To The 'No Free Lunch' Rule*, FORBES, Nov. 15, 2013, http://www.forbes.com/sites/realspin/2013/11/15/patent-trolls-are-the-economy-suffocating-exception-to-the-no-free-lunch-rule/ 68

FED. R. CIV. P. 8(a)(2) 64

FED. TRADE COMM'N, THE EVOLVING IP MARKETPLACE: ALIGNING PATENT NOTICE AND REMEDIES WITH COMPETITION (2011) 56, 63

Ga.-Pac. Corp. v. U.S. Plywood Corp., 318 F. Supp. 1116 (S.D.N.Y. 1970) 66

PHIL GOLDBERG, PROGRESSIVE POLICY INST., STUMPING PATENT TROLLS ON THE BRIDGE TO INNOVATION (2013) 56, 63

Robert P. Greenspoon, *Is the United States Finally Ready for a Patent Small Claims Court?*, 10 MINN. J.L. SCI. & TECH. 549 (2009), *available at* http://mjlst.umn.edu/prod/groups/ahc/@pub/@ahc/@mjlst/documents/asset/ahc_asset_366031.pdf 68

Innovation Act, H.R. 3309, 113th Cong. (as referred to Senate, Dec. 9, 2013) 61, 65, 68

John C. Jarosz & Michael J. Chapman, *The Hypothetical Negotiation and Reasonable Royalty Damages: The Tail Wagging the Dog*, 16 STAN. TECH. L. REV. 769 (2013), http://stlr.stanford.edu/pdf/royaltydamages.pdf 66

K-Tech Telecomms. v. Time Warner Cable, 714 F.3d 1277 (Fed. Cir. 2013) 65

Jim Kerstetter, *How Much Is that Patent Lawsuit Going to Cost You?*, CNET NEWS (Apr. 5, 2014), http://news.cnet.com/8301-32973_3-57409792-296/how-much-is-that-patent-lawsuit-going-to-cost-you/ 65, 68

Mark A. Lemley & Carl Shapiro, *Patent Holdup and Royalty Stacking*, 85 TEX. L. REV. 1991 (2007), http://faculty.haas.berkeley.edu/shapiro/stacking.pdf 66, 70

Brian J. Love & James C. Yoon, *Expanding Patent Law's Customer Suit Exception*, 93 B.U. L. REV. 1605 (2013), *available at* http://www.bu.edu/bulawreview/files/2013/10/LOVE-YOON_Expanding-Patent.pdf 60–62, 66

Macronix Int'l Co. v. Spansion Inc., No. 3:13-cv-679, 2014 U.S. Dist. LEXIS 31465 (E.D. Va. Mar. 10, 2014) 65

Md. Cas. Co. v. Pac. Coal & Oil Co., 312 U.S. 270 (1941) 68

Medimmune, Inc. v. Genentech, Inc., 549 U.S. 118 (2007) 67

Erin Mershon, *White House Aims to Undercut Patent Trolls*, POLITICO (Feb. 20, 2014), http://www.politico.com/story/2014/02/white-house-rolls-out-patent-actions-103727.html 63

Kimberly A. Moore, *Are District Court Judges Equipped to Resolve Patent Cases?*, 15 HARV. J.L. & TECH. 1 (2001) 67

Kimberly A. Moore, *Judges, Juries, and Patent Cases—An Empirical Peek Inside the Black Box*, 99 MICH. L. REV. 365 (2000) 67

Patent Abuse Reduction Act, S. 1013, 113th Cong. (2013) 65, 68

Patent Litigation and Innovation Act, H.R. 2639, 113th Cong. (2013) 62, 65

Patent Litigation Integrity Act, S. 1612, 113th Cong. (2013) 68

Patents Act 1990, ch. 12, sec. 133 (Austl.), *available at* http://www.austlii.edu.au/au/legis/cth/consol_act/pa1990109/ 68

PRICEWATERHOUSECOOPERS, 2013 PATENT LITIGATION STUDY: BIG CASES MAKE HEADLINES, WHILE PATENT CASES PROLIFERATE (2013), *available at* http://www.pwc.com/en_us/us/forensic-services/publications/assets/2013-patent-litigation-study.pdf 66, 68

Saving High-Tech Innovators from Egregious Legal Disputes Act, H.R. 845, 113th Cong. (2013) 68

Christopher B. Seaman, *Reconsidering the* Georgia-Pacific *Standard for Reasonable Royalty Patent Damages*, 2010 BYU L. REV. 1661, http://www.law2.byu.edu/lawreview/archives/2010/5/05Seaman.pdf 66

William H. Sorrell, Vt. Attorney Gen. & Jon Bruning, Neb. Attorney Gen., *Vermont and Nebraska Attorneys General Take Patent Trolls Head On*, NAAGAZETTE (Nat'l Ass'n of Attorneys Gen., Wash., D.C.), Oct. 29, 2013, *available at* http://www.naag.org/assets/files/pdf/gazette/7-9-10.Gazette.pdf 64

Thomas G. Southard & Paul F. Prestia, *Economics and Logic of Patent Litigation Versus Post Grant/Inter Partes Patent Review*, RATNER-PRESTIA (Oct. 3, 2012), *available at* http://ratnerprestia.com/220?article=485 67

The Impact of Patent Assertion Entities on Innovation and the Economy: Hearing Before the H. Subcomm. on Oversight and Investigations of the H. Comm. on Energy and Commerce, 113th Congress (2013) (statement of Charles Duan, Director, Patent Reform Project, Public Knowledge), *available at* http://docs.house.gov/meetings/IF/IF02/20131114/101483/HHRG-113-IF02-Wstate-DuanC-20131114.pdf 64

U.S. GOV'T ACCOUNTABILITY OFFICE, GAO-13-465, INTELLECTUAL PROPERTY: ASSESSING FACTORS THAT AFFECT PATENT INFRINGEMENT LITIGATION COULD HELP IMPROVE PATENT QUALITY (2013), *available at* http://www.gao.gov/assets/660/657103.pdf 60, 62–63, 65

U.S. PATENT & TRADEMARK OFFICE, MANUAL OF PATENT EXAMINING PROCEDURE (8th ed., 9th rev. 2012) 47–48, 54, 57–58, 67

Uniloc USA, Inc. v. Microsoft Corp., 632 F. 3d 1292 (Fed. Cir. 2011) . . 66

Stephen Wang, *The Impact of Patent Troll Demand Letters*, PUBLIC KNOWLEDGE (Nov. 13, 2013), http://www.publicknowledge.org/news-blog/blogs/impact-patent-troll-demand-letters 63

Maintaining Competition

David Balto, *Using the Antitrust Laws to Police Patent Privateering*, PATENTLY-O (June 3, 2013), http://patentlyo.com/patent/2013/06/guest-post-on-using-the-antitrust-laws-to-police-patent-privateering.html 70

eBay Inc. v. MercExchange, LLC, 547 U.S. 388 (2006) 70

Fed. Trade Comm'n v. Actavis, Inc., 133 S. Ct. 2223 (2013) 68–69

Herbert Hovenkamp, *Consumer Welfare In Competition And Intellectual Property Law*, 9 COMPETITION POL'Y INT'L 53 (2013) 69

Anne Layne-Farrar et al., *Pricing Patents for Licensing in Standard-Setting Organizations: Making Sense of FRAND Commitments*, 74 ANTITRUST L.J. 671 (2007) 69

Mark A. Lemley & Carl Shapiro, *A Simple Approach to Setting Reasonable Royalties for Standard-Essential Patents*, 28 BERKELEY TECH. L.J. 1135 (2013) 69

Mark A. Lemley & Carl Shapiro, *Patent Holdup and Royalty Stacking*, 85 TEX. L. REV. 1991 (2007), http://faculty.haas.berkeley.edu/shapiro/stacking.pdf 66, 70

Precision Instrument Mfg. Co. v. Auto. Maint. Mach. Co., 324 U.S. 806 (1945) 68

RPX Corp., Registration Statement (Form S-1) (Sept. 2, 2011) 70

U.S. DEP'T OF JUSTICE & FED. TRADE COMM'N, ANTITRUST ENFORCEMENT AND INTELLECTUAL PROPERTY RIGHTS: PROMOTING INNOVATION AND COMPETITION (2007), *available at* http://www.usdoj.gov/atr/public/hearings/ip/222655.pdf 69–70

U.S. Dep't of Justice & U.S. Patent & Trademark Office, *Policy Statement on Remedies for Standards-Essential Patents Subject to Voluntary F/RAND Commitments* (Jan. 8, 2013), http://www.justice.gov/atr/public/guidelines/290994.pdf 69

Walker Process Equip., Inc. v. Food Mach. & Chem. Corp., 382 U.S. 172 (1965) 68

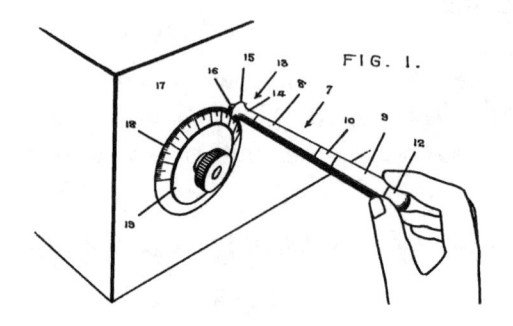

Colophon

This white paper is set in Cambria, with titles set in Ostrich Sans, a font designed by the League of Moveable Type. The cover was designed by Clarissa Ramon. The text was set using LaTeX, and the source code for the paper is available at https://github.com/PublicKnowledgeDC/patent-whitepaper.

This is the print edition of the paper, which differs from the original edition only in format and paper size.